DIVORCES
AND
NAMES CHANGED
IN MARYLAND

by Act of the Legislature

1634–1867

Mary K. Meyer

HERITAGE BOOKS
2007

HERITAGE BOOKS
AN IMPRINT OF HERITAGE BOOKS, INC.

Books, CDs, and more—Worldwide

For our listing of thousands of titles see our website
at
www.HeritageBooks.com

Published 2007 by
HERITAGE BOOKS, INC.
Publishing Division
65 East Main Street
Westminster, Maryland 21157-5026

International Standard Book Number: 978-1-58549-526-3

INTRODUCTION

Divorce in the Judeo-Christian culture dates from the Biblical era. It is first mentioned in the Book of Jeremiah, III:8, "I had put her away and given her a bill of divorcement." It was practiced widely in ancient Rome if we understand an old Roman epitaph correctly: "Seldom marriages last until death undivorced." Cato, Sulla, Pompey, Anthony, and Caesar were divorced and remarried from three to five times each.

After the Christian religion became the dominating influence in European life, interpretation of the Scriptures became both rigid and uniform but, while divorce was exceedingly rare within the Roman Catholic Church, there was never absolute prohibition in practice. Divorce or annulment could be arranged, provided money and power were available and just cause could be established.

It was not, therefore, without precedent that Henry VIII pleaded his suit for divorcement from Catharine of Aragon before the Pope. The shocking aspect of the case was not his attempt at divorce but rather his subsequent defiance of the Church when the divorce was denied.

Old English law recognized divorce a mensa et thoro, that is, divorce from bed and board. This remained the only type of judicial divorce until the middle of the nineteenth century and is referred to as judicial separation. In the United States it is usually referred to as legal separation.

Because Maryland and the majority of the American Colonies were from the outset settled mainly by emigrants from Great Britain, English law arrived in America with the colonists, therefore divorce was legal at the time of the founding of Maryland. And although divorce under English law was not a part of

iii

the common law but rather administered by the ecclesiastical courts, it too seems to have arrived in America with the colonists. Parliament could and did grant divorces before this time, however.

A study of the laws of Maryland does not reveal just when divorce a vinculo matromonii or absolute divorce became legal, leading one to believe it had been legal from the founding of the province. However, a thorough examination of the laws of Maryland does not reveal one case of legal separation or absolute divorce in the province during the colonial period as occurred in other colonies.

In 1658, one Robert Holt, of St. Mary's County entered into a second marriage with a certain Christian Bonnefield, Rev. William Wilkinson performing the ceremony. Wilkinson had previously drawn up and signed as a witness an agreement whereby Holt's first wife, Dorothy, released her husband from his marital obligations, stated she refused to be reconciled with him, confessed to two acts of adultery, and to having borne two bastard children. Holt was subsequently tried on a bigamy charge and Rev. Wilkinson as an accessory.[1]

In England absolute divorce could be granted by Parliament, so in Maryland by an act of the legislature. By the early 1800's the number of divorces increased, placing an increased burden on the state legislature. Perhaps it was for that reason a law was passed in 1829 delegating some of the authority in divorce suits to the county courts by allowing evidence to be taken by a county official. In a series of later laws, juris-

---

[1] *Archives of Maryland, Vol. 41, Proceedings of the Provincial Court, 1658-1662.* pp. 149-151, 228-230, 243, 244, 528. Raphael Semmes. *Crime and Punishment in Early Maryland,* Baltimore, The Johns Hopkins Press, 1938.

diction in divorce cases was ceded to the Chancellor and county courts as Courts of Equity by 1853.[2]

All too often the genealogist ignores divorce records in his quest for family history. He may do so under the impression that a divorce never occurred in his family, or because he does not know where such records can be found. These abstracts of divorce were copied from the published *Laws of Maryland*, a series of books which may be found in numerous libraries in Maryland as well as in some of the larger libraries (particularly law libraries) throughout the nation. There are complete sets at the Maryland Historical Society and The Enoch Pratt Free Library--both located in Baltimore, Maryland--and at the Maryland State Library in Annapolis, Maryland.

The various acts by which divorces were granted were by no means in standard form. Often the name of one of the parties or the residence of the parties was omitted. Women were often granted the right to resume their maiden names, but the maiden name was not always given. In the majority of cases grounds for the actions were not noted.

There has been no attempt to note here whether the decree was a legal separation or an absolute divorce. Should the reader wish to determine this point, he may obtain a copy of the complete act by which a particular divorce was granted.

The reader will note that in some cases a couple may seem to have been divorced twice. This is a case of first securing a decree a mensa et thoro, which prohibited either party from remarrying, then after a time if one or both parties wished to remarry, it was neces-

---

[2] *Laws of Maryland*, Chapter 202:1829, 128:1853, 262:1841, 245:1849.

sary to obtain a decree a vinculo matrimonii.

In some instances more complete accounts of these divorces can be found in the official recorded copy of the laws of Maryland which are available at the Hall of Records, Annapolis, Maryland. The same is true of the changes of names which are included in this work.

This work is not intended to be an "end all" of any individual's search for records of divorce or changes of names of Marylanders. It is intended only as a guide to self help. If there are errors herein--and it is quite impossible to do a work of this type without errors, despite checking and rechecking--the experienced researcher will understand and forgive, and he will always look at the original record.

Standard abbreviations, familiar to all genealogists, are used throughout. At the end of each entry two numbers appear. The first number indicates the chapter and the second indicates the session of the Legislature during which the act was passed. Where the abbreviation "sp." appears in parentheses, following these numbers, it indicates a special session of the legislature. On occasion, a notation such as Lib. #2, Fol. 343 appears in an entry. The first denotes the liber (book) and the second the folio (page) number of the official recorded copy of the laws of Maryland where the entry can be found.

For information on the location of divorce records in the various counties in Maryland, it is recommended the reader consult *The County Courthouses and Records of Maryland, Part II: The Records*, by Morris L. Radoff, Gust Skordas, Phebe R. Jacobsen. Publication No. 13, The Hall of Records Commission, State of Maryland, Annapolis, Maryland, 1963.

Mary Keysor Meyer
1969

DIVORCES AND NAMES CHANGED IN MARYLAND
1634-1854

ABELL, Jane, of Baltimore City, divorced from Benjamin H. Abell. 18 Feb. 1842 [110-1841]

ADALID, Michael, of Baltimore City, otherwise known as Michael Adalid Roderiguez and Rosella Adalid, marriage annulled and divorced. Children not to be illegitimated. 25 Jan. 1816 [157-1815]

ADAMS, Emeline R. See Emeline R. Hall.

ADAMS, Stephen, name changed to Stephen Henning Adams. 2 Feb. 1831 [36-1830]

ADAMS, Richard, of Talbot Co., divorced from Emeline P. Adams, late of Philadelphia, Pennsylvania, but now of the Territory of Wisconsin. 4 Mar. 1846 [251-1845]

ADREON, Christian. See Christian Sedgewick.

ADREON, George. See George Sedgewick.

ADREON, Jacob. See Jacob Sedgewick.

ADREON, Matthias. See Matthias Sedgewick.

ALDERSON, Charity, divorced from William C. Alderson, of Baltimore Co. She to use name of Charity Stansbury. She not to remarry. 22 Feb. 1831 [142-1803]

ALEXANDER, Archibald and Susanna entered into articles of separation, she taking charge of six children, two of whom were Alexander's. In July last, there was a well founded report he was dead, and believing he was dead, Susanna married John Muskett of Baltimore City. Marriage to Alexander annulled and divorced. Children not to be illegitimated. 25 Jan. 1806 [23-1805]

1

ALEXANDER, Jane Ashton. See Jane Ashton Callis.

ALEXANDER, William and Elizabeth, of Baltimore City, divorced. 21 Feb. 1826 [99-1825]

ALFORD, James, of Baltimore City, divorced from Jane Alford. 6 Feb. 1836 [48-1835]

ALLEN, Adeline, of Baltimore City, divorced from Alexander Allen. 12 Mar. 1840 [250-1839]

ALLEN, Wesleyana Elizabeth, infant daughter of Rev. John Allen, of Worcester Co., name changed to Ellen Ann Elzy Fontaine Allen. 29 Feb. 1840 [128-1847]

ALLISON, Jacob, divorced from Anna Allison. 26 Feb. 1840 [169-1839]

ALVEY, John Henry, child of Mrs. Anna McPherson Alvey, of St. Mary's Co., name changed to John Henry Cook. 14 Jan. 1841 [12-1840]

ALVEY, Ann Maria, child of Mrs. Anna McPherson Alvey, of St. Mary's Co., name changed to Ann Maria Cook. 14 Jan. 1841 [12-1840]

ALVEY, James Chapman, child of Mrs. Anna McPherson Alvey, of St. Mary's Co., name changed to James Chapman Cook. 14 Jan. 1841 [12-1841]

AMBROUSE, Ellen, of Washington Co., name changed to Elizabeth Ellen Shaw. 4 Mar. 1835 [132-1834]

ANDERSON, Anna Mary. See Anna Mary Coberth.

ANDERSON, Charles Thomas. See Charles Thomas Coberth.

ANDERSON, Francis Thomas. See Francis Thomas Coberth.

ANDREON, Mary Ann. See Mary Ann Fisher.

ANDREW, Curtis, of Caroline Co., divorced from Mary Jane Andrew. 9 Mar. 1850 [459-1849]

ANGELMEYER, Mathias, of Baltimore City, divorced from Christianna Angelmeyer. 9 Feb. 1842 [85-1841]

APPLEGARTH, James. See James Mills.

ARMSTRONG, Ann Elizabeth Amanda Christiana, divorced from Henry Armstrong, of St. Mary's Co. She to have custody of her child. 16 Mar. 1833 [210-1832]

ARNOLD, Benedict, of Baltimore City, name changed to George William Arnold. 6 Apr. 1841 [37-1841-sp.]

ARTHUR, Elizabeth, of Carroll Co., divorced from Joseph Arthur. 17 Mar. 1840 [301-1839]

ARTINSON, Rosanna, of Washington Co., divorced from Eli Artinson. 20 Mar. 1835 [307-1834]

ARTZ, Christian, of Frederick Co., name changed to Christian Burr Artz. 3 Mar. 1834 [131-1833]

ASKEY, Robert, of Harford Co., divorced from Margaret Askey. 17 Mar. 1840 [275-1839]

ATCHISON, Samuel Berry, of Charles Co., name changed to Samuel Atchison Berry. 20 Jan. 1798 [2-1797]

AULTHOUSE, Ann, of Baltimore City, divorced from Lewis Aulthouse. 13 Feb. 1840 [160-1839]

AUSTIN, William, of Baltimore City, divorced from Mary Austin. 14 Mar. 1839 [302-1838]

3

BACON, Benjamin W., of Baltimore City, divorced from Prudence Bacon. 10 Mar. 1837 [171-1836]

BAILEY, Mary. See Mary Snowden.

BAKER, Elizabeth, of Annapolis, divorced from William Baker. She to have custody of minor children. 23 Mar. 1836 [183-1835]

BAKER, Luther, of Baltimore City, name changed to Martin Luther Baker. 4 Jan. 1833 [2-1832]

BALDWIN, Mary, of Baltimore City, divorced from James Baldwin. 18 Mar. 1835 [240-1834]

BALDWIN, Sarah, of Harford Co., her husband, Taylor Baldwin, having lost his mind, speech, etc., she is granted and priveledged to rights as femme sole. 23 Feb. 1841 [163-1840]

BALL, Mary Ann, of Allegany Co., divorced from Jacob Ball. 14 Mar. 1834 [235-1833]

BALTZ, Isabella P., of Baltimore Co., divorced from John Baltz. 21 March 1835 [312-1834]

BALTZELL, Edward Buchanan, of Frederick Co., name changed to Edward Baltzell Buchanan. 1 Mar. 1852 [35-1852]

BANKS, Eleanor, of Baltimore City, divorced from Thomas Banks. 1 Feb. 1823 [140-1822]

BARKLEY, Mary Jane, of Baltimore City, married in 1849 to Joseph Barkley, releases all rights and demands she may have by virtue of the marriage. 1 Mar. 1854 [21-1854]

BARKS, John, of Washington Co., divorced from Mary Ramsburg Barks. 13 Feb. 1832 [105-1831]

BARLING, Elizabeth, and Joseph Barling, of Baltimore City, divorced. She to resume her maiden name, Pannel. 28 Mar. 1839 [300-1838]

BARNES, Abraham. See Abraham Barnes Mason.

BARNES, James and Mable Barnes, of Talbot Co., divorced. Children not to be illegitimated. Lib. TH #1, Fol. 514. 20 Jan. 1808 [166-1807]

BARNES, Maria, of Baltimore City, divorced from Richard H. Barnes. Neither party to remarry. 14 Mar. 1833 [231-1832]

BARNEY, John Holland. See George Stiles Dew.

BARNEY, Elizabeth Booth. See Elizabeth Booth.

BARNEY, William C. See Elizabeth Booth.

BARNUM, Sarah, of Baltimore City, David S. Barnum petitioned for divorce from Sarah Barnum and made certain charges. Sarah asks and is given divorce from David Strong Barnum. She to resume her maiden name (not given). See Sarah Gilmore. 27 Feb. 1830 [193-1829]

BARR, Charles, of Baltimore City, divorced from Margaret F. Barr. 27 Mar. 1839 [301-1838]

BARRET, Zaccheus, name changed to Zaccheus Onion. Lib. HS, Fol. 411. 24 Apr. 1762 [21-1762]

BARRETT, Sarah, of Baltimore City, divorced from Patrick Barrett. She to have custody of children. She not to remarry. 21 Mar. 1833 [272-1832]

5

BARRIERE, Charity F., of Baltimore City, divorced from David Barriere. 20 Feb. 1823 [170-1822]

BARROLL, William, of Kent Co., and Lucretia Barroll, marriage annulled. She living in adulterous state, separate from her husband. Issue not to be illegitimated. 20 Jan. 1798 [27-1797]

BARRON, Catharine Yustena, of Baltimore City, divorced from Joseph F. Barron. She to have custody of child. 13 Mar. 1839 [165-1838]

BAST, Barbara, of Frederick Co., divorced from Cornelius Bast. 2 Feb. 1830 [45-1829]

BATEMAN, William Lemuel, of Baltimore City, name changed to William Thomas Henry Worthington. 3 Mar. 1848 [174-1847]

BAXLEY, Levi and Margaret, of Baltimore City, marriage annulled and divorced. Children not to be illegitimated. 8 Jan. 1816 [63-1815]

BAYLEY, Mary Ann, of Dorchester Co., divorced from Josiah Bayley, Jr. She to resume her maiden name (not stated). 12 Jan. 1838 [5-1837]

BEAM, Mary Elizabeth. See Mary Elizabeth Willhide.

BEAMER, Susanna, of Baltimore City, divorced from Frederick Beamer. Children not to be illegitimated. 6 Jan. 1810 [50-1809]

BEARD, John. See Mary Manning.

BEATTY, Ann Margaret, of Washington Co. Control of Samuel Beatty annulled. She to have custody of children. 28 Jan. 1826 [42-1825]

6

BEAUZAMY, Emelie. See Emelie Berteau.

BECKER, Julia Ann, of Baltimore City, divorced from John H. Becker. 6 Mar. 1837. [132-1836]

BECKER, Julia Ann, of Baltimore City, divorced from John H. Becker. She to have custody of child/children. 14 Mar. 1838 [154-1837]

BECKLEY, Mary, of Washington Co., marriage to Henry Beckley annulled. 13 Mar. 1829 [176-1828]

BECKWITH, Maria W. B., of Talbot Co., divorced from Clement Beckwith. 16 Feb. 1821 [181-1820]

BELL, Caleb. See Caleb Smith.

BELLMAN, Henrietta, divorced from Henry Bellman. 9 Mar. 1850. (No residence given) [481-1849]

BELMEAR, Anna Maria, of Anne Arundel Co., divorced from Absalom Belmear. She to have custody of children. She and children to take and use surname of Waters. 6 Mar. 1834 [148-1833]

BENTZ, Catharine, of Washington Co., divorced from Adam Bentz. 20 Feb. 1826 [87-1825]

BENTZ, William. See William Snyder.

BERDEAU, Mary W., of Washington Co., divorced from Charles Berdeau. 17 Mar. 1837 [209-1836]

BERGER, Charles Frederick, of Baltimore City, divorced from Margaret Berger. 11 Mar. 1840 [240-1839]

BERRY, Catharine, of Baltimore City, divorced from William Berry. 19 Feb. 1841 [77-1840]

BERRY, Elisha. See Elisha Fergusson.

BERRY, Samuel Atchison. See Samuel Berry Atchison.

BERTEAU, Emelie, of Baltimore City, divorced from Peter Berteau. She to use her maiden name Beauzamy. 8 Mar. 1828 [129-1827]

BESORE, Mary, of Frederick Co., divorced from Jacob Besore. 24 Mar. 1836 [199-1835]

BILLINGSLEA, James, of Harford Co., divorced from Martha G.Billingslea. 6 Mar. 1850 [345-1849]

BLAKLEY, ELizabeth, of Baltimore Co., divorced from John Blakely. She to have custody of child by her present marriage. 6 Feb. 1827 [58-1826]

BLOCK, Sarah, of Dorchester Co., divorced from Arthur M. Block, of Baltimore City. 1 Feb. 1833 [20-1832]

BOMGARDNER, Elizabeth, of Frederick Co., divorced from Henry Bomgardner. 2 Feb. 1837 [47 -1836]

BOND, Mary E., of Baltimore City, divorced from William B. Bond. Neither party to remarry. 26 Feb.1833 [89-1832]

BOND, Thomas, of Baltimore City, name changed to Thomas Jackson Bond. 5 Jan. 1821 [26-1820]

BONAPARTE, Jerome and Elizabeth, of Baltimore City, marriage annulled. Child not to be illegitimated. Lib TH #3, Fol. 470. 15 Dec. 1812 (This is Betsey Patterson) [130-1812]

8

BONSACK, Nathaniel, of Frederick Co., divorced from Mary Bonsack. 12 Mar. 1840 [227-1839]

BOOTH, Elizabeth, of Newcastle, Delaware, m. 20 June 1845 to William C. Barney, of Baltimore City. He was to perform certain acts, according to a prenuptial agreement, before the marriage became legal, but failed to live up to the agreement. Divorce granted. 28 Jan. 1846 [44-1845]

BOOTH, William and Jane, marriage annulled. Children not to be illegitimated. 4 Jan. 1807 [69-1806]

BOOTS, Sarah, of Kent Co., name changed to Sarah Ingram. 4 Feb. 1840 [157-1839]

BOSS, Catharine, of Baltimore City, divorced from Samuel S. Boss. 15 Mar. 1834 [270-1833]

BOSS, Jerome, of Baltimore City, name changed to Jerome Boss White. 9 Mar. 1845 [6-1844]

BOSTETTER, Hannah, of Washington Co., declared femme sole. She vested with all title, etc. to property, both real and personal now in her possession. Henry Bostetter's liability annulled. 9 Mar. 1826 [226-1825]

BOSWORTH, James, of Baltimore City, marriage between he and Mary Amanda, infant daughter, under age 16, of Alexander Sandford, without parental consent, contrary to law (Chapter 12, Feb. 1777) annulled. She to resume name, Sandford. 20 Feb. 1827 [93-1826]

BOWEN, Aquila G., of Calvert Co., before his marriage to his present wife, Elizabeth, had two children born out of wedlock,

Octavius Wilkinson and George Wilkinson, by Rebecca Wilkinson, who has since died. He has taken the children to live with him and asks they be declared legitimate and their names changed to Bowen. So changed. 20 Jan. 1826 [17-1825]

BOWEN, Elizabeth, of Baltimore Co., divorced from Thomas Bowen. She to have custody of children. 13 Mar. 1827 [264-1826]

BOWIE, Catharine. See Catharine Johnson.

BOWIE, Hezekiah. See Hezekiah Johnson.

BOWIE, John A. See John A. Johnson.

BOWIE, Uriah. See Uriah Johnson.

BOWIE, Zachariah. See Zachariah Johnson.

BOWIE, John Truman Stoddert, name changed to John Truman Stoddert. 11 Feb. 1852 [7-1852]

BOYD, Eliza Ann, of Kent Co., divorced from James Boyd. 6 Mar. 1837 [124-1836]

BOYD, Joseph, of Prince George's Co., marriage to Elizabeth Boyd, annulled. She eloped from him in April 1801 and went to live with her parents, after about two weeks her persuaded her to return. She stayed until July then eloped again and never returned. In Spring of 1803 she went to London (sic) Co., Va. with a certain Thomas Donnell where she continued to live until August last, when she returned and has since been delivered of a child. She has requested a Justice of the Peace for Prince George's Co. to permit her to swear to a person in Virginia, thus avowing her adulterous conduct. The marriage is annulled and they are divorced. Any children born prior to 1803 not to be

illegitimated. Lib. TH #3, Fol. 415. 20
Jan. 1808

BOYER, John Wilmer Spencer. See John De Bentelo De Sylve.

BOYLAN, Thomas and Mary Good, (now Mary Gwinn)
marriage annulled and divorced. Her
marriage to John Gwinn, now deceased,
made valid. 20 Dec. 1808 (See Mary
Gwinn) [8-1808]

BRAND, William Flood, a native of Louisiana,
now a citizen of Maryland and resident of
Anne Arundel Co., name changed to William
Francis Brand. 4 Jan. 1845 [62-1844]

BRAY, Joseph, of Anne Arundel Co., marriage to
Anne Bray, annulled and they are divorced. She delivered of a Mulatto child
shortly after their marriage. 7 Jan.
1804 [94-1803]

BRERETON, Sarah A. See Sarah A. Dove.

BREWER, John, of Washington Co., name changed
to John Thomson Brewer. 28 Mar. 1836
[271-1835]

BRICE, Susan, of Baltimore City, divorced from
John P. Brice. 11 Mar. 1840 [236-1839]

BRITTINGHAM, Elijah, of Worcester Co., divorced from Julian Brittingham. 22 Jan.
1838 [16-1837]

BROMWELL, James, of Dorchester Co., born out
of wedlock. Known as Bromwell, sometimes
as Johnson. Name of Bromwell confirmed
to him, his wife, Mary Ann, and children,
Thomas, James, John Edward, William Wesley, and Levin Lake Bromwell. 17 Feb.
1835 [110-1834]

BROWN, Elizabeth M. and John C., articles of
separation confirmed. Articles dated 24

11

Sept. 1825 to be recorded in land records of Harford Co. within six months. 29 Jan. 1827 [44-1826]

BROWN, Edward Lewis, of Harford Co., name confirmed. 17 Jan. 1828 [9-1827]

BROWN, George Washington, of Harford Co., name confirmed. 17 Jan. 1828 [9-1827]

BROWN, Jehu, divorced from Elizabeth Brown. 18 Feb. 1848 [90-1847]

BROWNE, Joseph, of Kent Co., divorced from Mary Browne. 5 Mar. 1839 [133-1838]

BROWNING, Ellen, (no residence given), divorced from Louis H. Browning. She to have custody of children. She to use name of Ellen Lowry. 4 Mar. 1847 [212-1846]

BRYAN, Thomas Marsh Forman, name changed to Thomas Marsh Forman. 14 Jan. 1846 [21-1845]

BRYAN, Florida, wife of Thomas Marsh Forman Bryan, name changed to Florida Forman. 14 Jan. 1846 [21-1845]

BUCHANAN, Edward Baltzell. See Edward Buchanan Baltzell.

BULL, Ann S., of Baltimore Co., name changed to Ann S. Preston. 4 Feb. 1841 [33-1840]

BULL, Fanny M., of Baltimore Co., name changed to Fanny M. Preston. 4 Feb. 1841 [33-1840]

BULL, Henry D., of Baltimore Co., name changed to Henry D. Preston. 4 Feb. 1841 [33-1840]

BULL, Mary E., of Baltimore Co., name changed to Mary E. Preston, 4 Feb. 1841 [33-1840]

BURK, Thomas and Elizabeth, of Frederick Co., marriage annulled and divorced. Children not to be illegitimated. Lib. TH #2, Fol. 55. 6 Jan. 1810 [13-1809]

BURKE, Ada. See Ada Hopkins.

BURKE, Josephine. See Josephine Hopkins.

BURKE, Sarah E. F. See Sarah E. F. Hopkins.

BUSH, Anna Maria, of Baltimore City, divorced from Robert Bush, of Baltimore City. She to have custody of her child. 12 Mar. 1827 [238-1826]

BUSICK, Samuel Jump. See Samuel Busick Jump.

BUSICK, Senah. See Samuel Busick Jump.

BUTLER, Courtney Ann, of Baltimore City, divorced from Mansfield Butler. 14 Feb. 1839 [127-1838]

BUTTON, Mary Ann. See James W. James.

BYWATERS, William, of Baltimore City, divorced from Ann Bywaters. 12 Mar. 1840 [228-1839]

CAHALL, Joseph B., illegitimate child of Joseph B. Perry, of Talbot Co., name changed to Joseph B. Perry. 23 Feb. 1839 [80-1838]

CAHALL, William Henry, illegitimate son of Joseph B. Perry, of Talbot Co., name changed to William Henry Perry. 23 Feb. 1839 [80-1838]

CAHALL, Sarah, of Caroline Co., divorced from John Cahall. 21 Jan. 1821 [133-1820]

CALAHAN, Margaret, of Frederick Co., divorced from Patrick Calahan. 16 Mar. 1835 [221-1834]

CALDWELL, William, of Baltimore City, formerly of Harford Co., name changed to William Quarll Caldwell. 3 Apr. 1841 [12-1841 (sp)]

CALLIS, Otho Williams, divorced from Jane Ashton Callis. She to resume her maiden name, Jane Ashton Alexander. She not to remarry. 5 Feb. 1830 [59-1829]

CANNON, Anne R., of Baltimore City, divorced from John W. Cannon. 2 Mar. 1837 [110-1836]

CAPLE, Jacob. See Jacob Cole.

CAPLE, Samuel. See Samuel Cole.

CAPLE, William. See William Cole.

CAREY, George, of Worcester Co., divorced from Nancy Carey. 16 Mar. 1840 [262-1839]

CARLEN, James. See William Sentee.

CARLEN, William. See William Sentee.

CARNAN, Charles Ridgely, nephew of Capt. Charles Ridgely, of Baltimore Co., deceased, and his son, Charles, names changed to Ridgely, according to will of Capt. Charles Ridgely, and to bear coat-of-arms and armorial bearings of Ridgely family. 14 Dec. 1790 [10-1790]

CARNAN, Charles Ridgely, name had been changed to Charles Ridgely (see 10-1790) and also the names of his children, including females. 31 Dec. 1801 [78-1801]

CARNAN, Thomas, of Baltimore City, confined upwards of ten months in Baltimore Co. gaol, having been tried on 2nd Monday Jan. 1809, and convicted of begetting an illegitimate child on body of Elizabeth

14

Daffell. Released from gaol. 6 Jan. 1810 [157-1809]

CARR, Francis Wakeman, of Harford Co., name changed to Francis Carr Smith. 4 May 1852 [211-1852]

CARROLL, Charles Tucker. See Charles Carroll Tucker.

CARROLL, James. See James Macubbin.

CARROLL, Nicholas. See Nicholas Macubbin.

CARTY, Edward, of Kent Co., divorced from Mary Ann Carty. 27 Feb. 1850 [291-1849]

CASE, John L., of Queen Anne's Co., name changed to John Lewis Cass. 28 Feb. 1844 [187-1843]

CASS, John Lewis. See John L. Case.

CASSELL, Catharine. See Peter Rouck.

CASSELL, Elizabeth. See Peter Rouck.

CASSELL, Eve. See Peter Rouck.

CASSELL, Sarah. See Peter Rouck.

CECIL, Ann, of Queen Anne's Co., divorced from John Cecil. 9 Mar. 1841 [224-1840]

CHAMBERS, Ezekiel F., and Sarah G. Chambers, of Kent Co., divorced. 9 Feb. 1836. [87-1835]

CHAMBERS, Julianna. See Julianna Wooters.

CHANGEUR, Josephine, of Baltimore City, marriage to Jean Changeur, annulled and divorced. Children not to be illegitimated. Lib. TH #2, Fol. 374. 6 Jan. 1810 [158-1809]

15

CHAPMAN, Ann, divorced from Job Chapman, of
    Baltimore Co. She not to remarry. 20
    Mar. 1835 [314-1834]

CHARLES, John and Betsey CHarles, of Talbot
    Co., divorced. 20 Feb. 1830 [104-1829]

CHAVALIER, Eliza, of Baltimore City, divorced
    from Nicholas W. Chavalier. She to have
    custody of child/children. 24 Mar. 1836
    [293-1825]

CHAVALIER, Eliza vs. Nicholas W. Chavalier,
    second section of above act (293-1835)
    repealed and Nicholas is given custody of
    child/children. 3 June 1836 [389-1835]

CHRIST, John, of Frederick Co., divorced from
    Susannah Christ. She delivered of a
    Mulatto child. 31 Dec. 1801 [65-1801]

CLAGGETT, Ann Elizabeth, daughter of Thomas W.
    Claggett, of Prince George's Co., name
    changed to Susan Guiger Harry Claggett.
    6 Mar. 1846 [316-1845]

CLAGGETT, Catharine, daughter of John H. Clag-
    gett, of Prince George's Co., name
    changed to Ida Sophia Claggett. 28 May
    1853 [331-1853]

CLAGGETT, Harriet. See Harriet Woodward.

CLAGGETT, James. See James Woodward.

CLARK, Eliza A., of Frederick Co., divorced
    from Samuel C. Clark. 1 Mar. 1842 [179-
    1841]

CLARKE, George Augustus, of Allegany Co., name
    changed to George Augustus Duncan Clarke.
    11 Jan. 1843 [6-1842]

CLARKE, John, of Caroline Co., divorced from
    Ruth Clarke. 17 Feb. 1825 [121-1824]

CLARKE, Marsilina, divorced from Baly R. Clarke. 14 Mar. 1839 [293-1838]

CLAYTON, Isaac Smith. See Isaac Smith.

CLERK, James and Margaret Russell Clerk, his wife, of Prince George's Co.; her aunt, Miss Eleanor Anne Lee, has no offspring, and desires James and Margaret to assume name of Clerk Lee. Right granted and also right to bear coat-of-arms and armorial bearings of the Lee family. 7 Jan. 1804 [69-1803]

CLINGAN, Andrew Jackson. See Andrew Jackson Guyton.

COBERTH, Anna Mary, of Calvert Co., name changed to Anna Mary Anderson. 27 May 1853 [312-1853]

COBERTH, Charles Thomas, of Calvert Co., name changed to Charles Thomas Anderson. 27 May 1853 [312-1853]

COBERTH, Francis Thomas, of Calvert Co., name changed to Francis Thomas Anderson. 27 May 1853 [312-1853]

COCHRAN, Charlotte, of Baltimore City, name changed to Charlotte Cochran Irvine. Lib. TH #3, Fol. 362. 25 Nov. 1812 [31-1812]

COCHRAN, Henry, of Baltimore City, name changed to Henry Cochran Irvine. Lib. TH #3, Fol. 362. 25 Nov. 1812 [21-1812]

CODET, Joseph R., of Baltimore City, divorced from Julia Ann Codet. 9 Mar. 1848 [260-1847]

CODLING, Ann Maria, of Baltimore Co., name changed to Mary Ann Maria Lewis. 9 Jan. 1841 [13-1840]

COGGESHALL, Ann. See Ann E. B. Sigler.

COLE, Jacob, name changed to Jacob Caple. Samuel Caple represents that previous to his marriage with Mary Cole, they had three sons, Jacob, Samuel, and William. Since their marriage they had had several daughters. He asks that the sons names be changed to Caple in order that they may have the same suname as their father. 6 Jan. 1810 [4-1809]

COLE, Mary, name changed to Mary Caple. See Jacob Cole. 6 Jan. 1810 [4-1809]

COLE, Samuel, name changed to Samuel Caple. See Jacob Cole. 6 Jan. 1810 [4-1809]

COLE, Stephen, name changed to Gill. He was born prior to marriage of his father, Stephen Gill to his mother, whose maiden name was Cole. 26 Dec. 1794 [36-1794]

COLE, William, name changed to William Caple. See Jacob Cole. 6 Jan. 1810 [4-1809]

COLEGATE, Edward, of Baltimore City, divorced from Ann Colegate. 13 Mar. 1839 [180-1838]

COLEMAN, Julian, of Baltimore City, divorced from Edward Coleman. She to have custody of son, Thomas Kenedy Coleman. 20 Feb. 1824 [158-1823]

COLGAN, Joseph S. See Joseph S. Colgar.

COLGAR, Joseph S., mistake made in his name, it was written Colgan. Error corrected. 14 Feb. 1821 [169-1820]

COLLINS, Emily, of Baltimore City, divorced from James C. Collins. 2 Mar. 1850 [344-1849]

COLLINS, James W., of Baltimore City, divorced from Sarah Collins. 20 Feb. 1834 [123-1833]

COLVIN, Richard. See Richard Warford.

CONNELLY, William, of Dorchester Co., name changed to William Smoot. 9 Mar. 1827 [187-1826]

CONNER, ELiza, of Baltimore City, divorced from Joseph Conner. 9 Mar. 1850 [443-1849]

CONWAY, Rebecca, of Baltimore City, divorced from Thomas P. Conway. 22 Feb. 1850 [138-1849]

COOK, Anna Maria. See Anna Maria Alvey.

COOK, James Chapman. See James Chapman Alvey.

COOK, John Henry. See John Henry Alvey.

COOK, Nancy, of Carroll Co., divorced from Rezin Cook. She to have custody of daughter, Susan Ann Cook. 30 Jan. 1840 [199-1839]

COOKE, Robert, of Queen Anne's Co., name changed to Robert Cooke Tilghman. His uncle, Col. Richard Tilghman devised to him if he should use surname Tilghman. Lib. TH #2, Fol. 581. 24 Dec. 1810 [111-1810]

COOPER, Joseph, of Baltimore Co., divorced from Nancy Cooper. 9 Mar. 1850 [450-1849]

COOPER, Mahaly, of Caroline Co., declared femme sole. Liability of William A. Cooper annulled. She to have custody of children. 17 Feb. 1826 [75-1825]

COPPAGE, Freeborn. See Freeborn Coppage Dodson.

CORKRAN, James Francis, child of Nancy Corkran of Caroline Co., surname changed to Love. 28 Jan. 1839 [26-1838]

CORKRAN, Thomas Henry, child of Nancy Corkran of Caroline Co., surname changed to Love. 28 Jan. 1839 [26-1838]

CORNER, Mary, of Dorchester Co., divorced from Solomon Corner. She not to remarry. 22 Jan. 1838 [12-1837]

COTNER, Dion, of Caroline Co., name changed to Dion Downes. 7 Dec. 1816 [6-1816]

COUDY, Catharine. See Catharine Maker.

COUDY, James. See Catharine Maker.

COUDY, Mahala. See Catharine Maker.

COYLE, Catharine, of Cecil Co., divorced from Terrence Coyle. 22 Mar. 1836 [344-1835]

CRADOCK, John. See John Walker.

CRADOCK, Thomas. See Thomas Walker.

CRAIN. See also Crane.

CRAIN, Margaret, of Baltimore City, marriage to Thomas Crain annulled and divorced. Children not to be illegitimated. Lib. TH #2, Fol. 589. 24 Dec. 1810 [113-1810]

CRALL, Samuel, of Washington Co., divorced from Elizabeth Crall. 31 Mar. 1841 [7-1841 (sp)]

CRAMER, John P., of Frederick Co., divorced from Sophia Cramer. 9 Mar. 1847 [243-1846]

CRANE, John. See Mary Maginnis.

CRAWFORD, John. See John Mills.

CREIGHTON, Samuel Raitt, name changed to Samuel Raitt Keene. 19 Feb. 1833 [68-1832]

CRESAP, Phebe, of Allegany Co., divorced from John M. Cresap. 29 Jan. 1819 [94-1818]

CRISFIELD, John Woodland, infant son of John W. Crisfield, of Somerset Co., name changed to Henry Page. 21 Feb. 1844 [143-1843]

CROMWELL, Benjamin, of Baltimore Co., authority and control over Julia Ann Cromwell, his wife, annulled. She to have custody of infant daughter. Benjamin not responsible for support of child. 17 Feb. 1825 [114-1824]

CROPPER, James, alias James McCollester, of Dorchester Co., was born out of wedlock. His mother was a McCollester, his father was a Cropper. Name established as Cropper. 6 Feb. 1823 [114-1822]

CROWL, William, of Baltimore Co., authority over Rosanna Crowl, his wife, annulled. 17 Feb. 1825 [117-1824]

CRUM, Mrs. William. See Margaret Razer.

CUDJO, Edward, grandchild of Joseph Cudjo of Kent Co. [120-1817]

CUDJO, James, illegitimate son of Joseph Cudjo of Kent Co., and Joseph's grandchildren, Edward and Richard Cudjo. Title to land confirmed and made valid. 4 Feb. 1818 [120-1817]

CUDJO, Joseph. See James Cudjo. [120-1817]

CUDJO, Richard, grandchild of Joseph Cudjo of Kent Co. [120-1817]

CULLEMBER, Ann, wife of John Cullember, of Calvert Co., name changed to Ann Williams. 5 Jan. 1827 [3-1826]

CULLEMBER, John, of Calvert Co., surname changed to Williams. John was born out of wedlock, his mother Mary Cullember, is since dead, and he hath assumed the name of Williams, married and hath a child. 5 Jan. 1827 [3-1826]

CULLEMBER, Mary Ann, daughter of John and Ann Cullember, of Calvert Co., name changed to Williams. 5 Jan. 1827 [3-1826]

CULLEMBER, Lewis, of Calvert Co., name changed to Lewis Harrison. 22 Feb. 1830 [124-1829]

CULVERWELL, Ann, of Baltimore City, divorced from William Culverwell. She to have custody of child by her present marriage. 7 Feb. 1827 [62-1826]

CUMMING, Araminta. See Ely Dorsey.

CUNNINGHAM, John Amos, of Frederick Co., name changed to John Amos Hosselbock Cunningham. 27 May 1853 [313-1853]

CUNNINGHAM, Martha Elizabeth, of Harford Co., divorced from Mortimer Cunningham. She to have custody of children. 27 Feb. 1832 [134-1831]

CURRAN, Catharine, of Baltimore City, divorced from John Curran. 5 Apr. 1839 [364-1838]

CURRY, Sarah, of Frederick Co., divorced from James Currey. Her name changed to Sarah Dods. 10 Mar. 1828 [147-1827]

CUYCK, Abraham, of Baltimore City, divorced from Susan L. Cuyck. 7 Mar. 1840 [326-1839]

DAFFELL, Elizabeth. See Thomas Carnan.

DANSKIN, Margaret, of Baltimore City, divorced from William Danskin. 11 Feb. 1820 [146-1819]

DANSKIN, Maria, of Baltimore City, divorced from Washington A. Danskin. 13 Mar. 1839 [175-1838]

DARRINGTON, Mary Ann, of Baltimore City, divorced from William D. Darrington. She to have custody of children by her present marriage. 13 Mar. 1827 [258-1826]

DASHIELL, Theodore Gunby. See Theodore Gunby.

DAVID, Eliza, divorced from Victor David. 28 Feb. 1834 [104-1833]

DAVIDSON, Lewis Grant, formerly Lewis Grant. By last will and testament of uncle, Samuel Davidson, of District of Columbia, he was to change his name to Davidson. The name confirmed to him. 23 Dec. 1810 [20-1810]

DAVIS, David. See David Davis Pagett.

DAVIS, Henry and Caroline Matilda Davis, of Baltimore City, divorced. Children not to be illegitimated. 19 Feb. 1831 [133-1830]

DAVIS, Jerimiah Perry. See Jerimiah Perry.

DAVIS, Mary, of Washington Co., divorced from John Davis. She to have custody of children. 3 Feb. 1827 [54-1826]

DAVIS, William Smith. See Jerimiah Perry.

23

DAWSON, George, of Caroline Co., divorced from Rebecca Dawson. 12 Mar. 1827 [233-1826]

DAWSON, Thomas, of Dorchester Co., name changed to Thomas McKenzie. 29 Jan. 1836 [36-1835]

DEAL, Mary. See Mary Grimes.

DEAL, Peter. See Mary Grimes.

DEBRULER, Mary, of Frederick Co., divorced from James C. Debruler. 21 Feb. 1829 [73-1828]

DECOURTRES, Louisa, name changed to Louisa Jacobs, adopted by George Jacobs, silver-smith and jeweler, of Baltimore City. 21 Feb. 1825 [150-1824]

DEEMS, Francis M., of Allegany Co., divorced from Parmelia Deems. 5 Mar. 1850 [308-1849]

DEFORD, John, of Queen Anne's Co., name confirmed. Mistakenly called Edward Deford; has an afflicted son, Thomas Deford. 8 Feb. 1823 [113-1822]

DELAHAY, Henry, the younger, son of Henry Delahay, the elder, of Talbot Co., declared legitimate. About 1796, Henry, the elder cohabited with Susan Millington, and from that time on until her death, and had issue, Henry, the younger, James, and Robert. 9 Mar. 1827 [196-1826]

DELHAY, James, son of Henry Delahay, declared legitimate. See above. 9 Mar. 1827 [196-1826]

DELAHAY, Robert, son of Henry Delahay, declared legitimate. See above. 9 Mar. 1827 [196-1826]

DEMMETT. See also Dimmitt.

DEMMETT, Catharine, name changed to Catharine
Ringold. Lib. TH #2, Fol. 53. 23 Dec.
1808 [57-1808]

DEMMETT, James W. and Catharine, marriage
annulled and divorced. They married
about six years ago and had two daughters. He attempted suicide by cutting
his throat, threatens life of petitioner,
she lives in hourly danger, he is in
continual state of intoxication. 4 Jan.
1807 [76-1806]

DENSON, Manaen B., of Baltimore City, divorced
from Theresa Ann Denson. 12 Mar. 1836
[167-1835]

DERR, Eve. See Conrad Holtzmann.

DE SYLVE, John De Bentelo, of Kent Co., name
changed to John Wilmer Spencer Boyer. 16
Dec. 1818 [86-1818]

DEW, George Stiles, a minor, of Baltimore
City, name changed to John Holland Barney. 1 Mar. 1826 [185-1825]

DE YOUNG, Michael and Mary De Young, marriage
annulled and divorced. Children born
before June next not to be illegitimated.
2 Feb. 1827 [50-1826]

DICKEHUT, Margaret Mitchell, of Baltimore
City, divorced from Henry F. Dickehut.
She to have custody of child, Margaret
Lyford Dickehut. She and child to take
surname, Lyford. 23 Mar. 1838 [347-1837]

DICKINSON, Henry and Anne, his wife, of Caroline Co., presented to Grand Jury, for
marriage within degree of affinity al-
lowed by law. Had issue. Marriage declared valid. No date given. [6-1784]

DIDIER, Jane, of Baltimore City, divorced from Jefferson Didier. She to have custody of children. 25 Jan. 1837 [90-1836]

DIMMITT, Caroline, of Baltimore City, divorced from Washington Dimmitt. 26 Feb. 1840 [170-1839]

DIXON, Albert Francis, of Prince George's Co., name changed to Albert Francis Jenkins. 27 Jan. 1853 [1-1853]

DODS, Sarah. See Sarah Currey.

DODSON, Eliza, of St. Michael's, Talbot Co., married Terrence Dooris, a native of Ireland, but the marriage proved illegal and void. She bore two children by him, Margaret Ann and William Terrence. Surnames changed to Dooris, as he willed her property, etc. 8 Jan. 1824 [47-1823]

DODSON, Freeborn Coppage, a minor, of Queen Anne's Co., name changed to Freeborn Coppage. 22 Feb. 1826 [101-1825]

DOLAN, John, of Baltimore City, divorced from Margaret Dolan. 22 Mar. 1836 [343-1835]

DONALDSON, James Lowry. See James Donaldson Lowry.

DONALDSON, Julianna, of Cecil Co., divorced from William B. Donaldson. Neither to remarry. 28 Jan. 1833 [21-1832]

DONALDSON, Julianna, divorced from William B. Donaldson. She to have custody of children and they are not to be illegitimated. See also above. 14 Mar. 1834 [230-1833]

DONNELL, Thomas. See Joseph Boyd.

DOORIS, Eliza. See Eliza Dodson.

DOORIS, Margaret Ann. See Eliza Dodson.

DORRIS, Terrence. See Eliza Dodson.

DORRIS, William Terrence. See Eliza Dodson.

DORNEY, Harriet, of Harford Co., divorced from Henry Dorney. 21 Mar. 1837 [286-1836]

DORSEY, Ely, of Ely Dorsey, of Frederick Co., and Araminta Cumming, of Anne Arundel Co., marriage articles, dated 26 Jan. 1801, recorded in General Court Records. Bk. JG #6, pp. 117, 118, made valid. 15 Jan. 1808 [5-1807]

DORSEY, Rachel, of Frederick Co., divorced from Benjamin Dorsey. 24 Feb. 1841 [120-1840]

DOVE, Sarah A., of Prince George's Co., divorced from William Dove. She to resume her maiden name, Sarah Ann Brereton. 1 Mar. 1842 [166-1841]

DOVELIN, Henry, of Baltimore Co., name changed to Henry John Hawkins. 12 Feb. 1847 [52-1846]

DOWLING, Eliza Jane, divorced from William Dowling, of Prince George's Co. 10 Mar. 1846 [388-1845]

DOWNER, Frances Ida. See Frances Ida Sicard.

DOWNES, Dion. See Dion Cotner.

DOWSON, George, of Caroline Co., marriage to Rebecca Dowson, annulled. 12 Mar. 1827 [233-1826]

DRAKE, Ann H., of Baltimore City, divorced from Matthew Drake. Neither to remarry. 17 Feb. 1832 [57-1831]

DRAKE, Thomas and Martha Drake, of Kent Co.,
marriage annulled and divorced. Children
not to be illegitimated. 8 Jan. 1816
[66-1815]

DUDLEY, Alexander Ewing. See Alexander Ewing.

DUKES, Mary, of Worcester Co., divorced from
John Dukes. 10 Mar. 1841 [244-1840]

DYERMAN, Mary Jane, of Washington Co., divorced from James H. Dyerman. 9 Mar. 1850
[444-1849]

EASTERDAY, Jacob, of Washington Co., divorced
from Fanny Easterday. 6 Feb. 1836 [46-
1835]

EBRECHT, Mary, of Washington Co., authority of
her husband, Henry Ebrecht, annulled.
Her father, John Mayer, of Washington
Co., lately died intestate. 28 Jan. 1826
[89-1825]

ECHER, John and Hannah Myers, or Echer, marriage contract made valid. She and issue
entitled to certain privileges, etc. 11
Mar. 1837 [177-1836]

EDWARDS, William, of Kent Co., divorced from
Mary E. Edwards. 3 Feb. 1842 [58-1841]

ELLICOTT, Louisa, of Baltimore City, divorced
from Thomas Ellicott, Jr. She to have
custody of children. 20 Feb. 1840 [191-
1839]

ELLIOTT, Sarah, of Baltimore City, divorced
from Grafton W. Elliott. 3 Feb. 1842
[57-1841]

ELVINS, Caroline R., of Baltimore City, divorced from William Elvins. 25 Feb. 1825
[177-1824]

ELWORTHY, Josephine Street, of Annapolis, divorced from Richard James Hawke. (See Josephine Hawke.) 9 Feb. 1842 [86-1841]

ELY, Hannah J. D., of Baltimore City, divorced from Juda Ely. She to resume her maiden name, Fearson. She to have custody of child/children. 2 Mar. 1837 [107-1836]

EMMONS, Ira and Zilpha Emmons, of Cecil Co., divorced. 23 Feb. 1830 [148-1829]

EMORY, Peregrine and Kitty E., of Queen Anne's Co., divorced. Children not to be illegitimated. 8 Jan. 1816 [60-1815]

ENNIS, Mary Ann. See Mary Ann Farrell.

ENTLEY, Michael and Mary Entley, of Allegany Co., marriage annulled and divorced. Children not to be illegitimated. 20 Dec. 1815 [20-1815]

ENSOR, Luke (of William), and Rachel Ensor, of Baltimore City, marriage annulled. One half the money from sale of property devised to Rachel by her father, Darby Ensor, to be paid to her and one half to her minor child, etc. 31 Jan. 1829 [13-1828]

ERICKSON, Elizabeth. See David Jones.

ERICKSON, Mary. See David Jones.

ESTEP, Richard Tillard. See Richard Tillard.

ETHERINGTON, Susan C., of Baltimore (city or county not stated), divorced from John Etherington. 10 Mar. 1841 [249-1840]

EVANS, Anna Maria, of Baltimore Co., divorced from Daniel Evans. 12 Mar. 1840 [251-1839]

EVANS, Charles. See Charles Ricketts.

EVANS, Charles Augustus Kerr, infant son of Alexander S. Evans, of Somerset Co., name changed to Charles Augustus Polk Evans. 7 Mar. 1850 [383-1849]

EVANS, Richard Penhallow, of Anne Arundel Co., name changed to Richard Stewart Evans. 23 Mar. 1839 [217-1838]

EVERLY, Emma Olivia, of Washington Co., name changed to Emma Olivia Martin. 6 Mar. 1850 [400-1849]

EVERITT, William B., of Kent Co., divorced from Emily F. Everitt. 19 Feb. 1835 [115-1834]

EWING, Alexander, a minor, of Talbot Co., name changed to Alexander Ewing Dudley. 1 Feb. 1827 [47-1826]

EYERS, George Washington. See Nathan Nicholson.

FARRELL, Mary Ann, divorced from James U. Farrell. She to resume her maiden name, Ennis, and not to remarry. 15 Mar. 1834 [250-1833]

FARRELL, Mary Ann, of Baltimore City, divorced from James W. Farrell. (See above.) 25 Mar. 1839 [236-1838]

FARRIN, Eliza. See Eliza Selby.

FARROW, Charles and Ann Farrow, marriage annulled and divorced. Lib. TH #2, Fol. 189. 9 June 1809 [12-1809 (sp)]

FEARSON, Hannah. See Hannah Ely.

FECHTIG, Sally Ann Post, of Washington Co., name changed to Sarah Ann Post. (This was repealed. See Sarah Ann Post, 126-1846). 16 Mar. 1840 [293-1839]

FEEZER, Eve, of Frederick Co., divorced from
Joseph Feezer. She to have custody of
children by her present marriage. 28
Jan. 1826 [43-1825]

FELL, John Sands. See John Sands Fell Stoddard.

FERGUSON. See also Furgusson.

FERGUSON, Benjamin and Ruth Ferguson, of "Cae-
cil" Co., marriage annulled. He to pay
$35.00 per year to Ruth. Children not to
be illegitimated. 4 Jan. 1807 [77-1806]

FERGUSON, Henrietta M., of Cecil Co., divorced
from William Ferguson. Son, John, is
mentioned in will of John Edward Ferguson, Sr., late of Cecil Co. Henrietta is
heir of Benjamin Porter, late of Cecil
Co., etc. Son, John, not to be illegitimated. 11 Feb. 1836 [88-1835]

FINROCK, Elizabeth, of Frederick Co., divorced
from John Jacob Finrock. The executor of
Henry Finrock, late of Frederick Co., deceased, to pay over to Elizabeth Finrock,
granddaughter of said Henry, amount due
her from Henry's will. 1 Mar. 1832 [152-
1831]

FISH, Eliza, of Cecil Co., divorced from John
Fish. 10 Feb. 1825 [122-1824]

FISH, Henrietta. See Henrietta Reid.

FISHER, Hannah C. See Hannah C. Pierce.

FISHER, Mary Ann R., of Dorchester Co., divorced from Levin T. Fisher. 3 Apr. 1841
[15-1841 (sp)]

FISHER, Mary Ann, of Baltimore City, name
changed to Mary Ann Anderson. 6 Mar.
1850 [352-1849]

FITZHUGH, ELizabeth S., of Baltimore City, control over her by her husband, John Fitzhugh, of Calvert Co., annulled. 25 Jan. 1819 [56-1818]

FLEMING, Anne, of Worcester Co., divorced from Henry Fleming. 1 Mar. 1842 [160-1841]

FLETCHER, Samuel James, of Baltimore Co., divorced from Anne Powne Fletcher. 10 Mar. 1842 [334-1841]

FLING, Rebecca. See Rebecca Wilson. See also Rebecca King.

FLOYD, Jemima, of St. Mary's Co., divorced from Jesse Floyd. 20 Feb. 1824 [159-1823]

FLOYD, Mary, of St. Mary's Co., divorced from Joseph Floyd. 6 Feb. 1836 [47-1835]

FOGG, Judson J., of Baltimore City, name changed to Judson Gilman. 16 Jan. 1844 [31-1843]

FORD, Achsah Cocky, of Baltimore Co., name changed to Achsah Cocky Deye Ford. 14 Jan. 1848 [16-1847]

FORD, William, of Montgomery Co., divorced from Acenia Ford. 8 Feb. 1836 [43-1835]

FOREMAN, Susan, of Queen Anne's Co., divorced from John S. Foreman. 26 Mar. 1836 [207-1835]

FORMAN, Florida. See Florida Bryan.

FORMAN, Thomas Marsh. See Thomas Marsh Forman Bryan.

FOWLER, Mary Ann, of Baltimore City, divorced from Benjamin Fowler. 3 Apr. 1841 [14-1841 (sp)]

FRANCISCUS, Albert G., of Baltimore City, divorced from Eliza J. Franciscus. 18 Mar. 1833 [248-1832]

FRANK, Susanna, of Baltimore City, divorced from Gustavus Frank. 19 Feb. 1841 [87-1840]

FREEMAN, Jane, of Annapolis, divorced from William L. Freeman. Neither to remarry. 14 Mar. 1832 [320-1831]

FRENCH, Ann G., of Baltimore City, divorced from Thomas French. 14 Mar. 1834 [248-1833]

FRESHOUR, Catherine, of Frederick Co., divorced from Jacob Freshour. 4 Feb. 1818 [123-1817]

FRIDLEY, Catharine, of Washington Co., divorced from Andrew Fridley. She to have custody of her child, Jacob Fridley. 3 Feb. 1823 [88-1823]

FULLMER, John Jackson, a native of Pennsylvania, now a resident of Maryland, name changed to John Jackson Lutts. 18 Mar. 1853 [72-1853]

FURGUSSON, ELisha, of Prince George's Co., name changed to Elisha Berry. Lib. TH #3, Fol. 139. 27 Dec. 1811 [125-1811]

FURNISS, Ephraim and Polly Furniss, of Somerset Co., marriage annulled. Polly was delivered of a Mulatto child Sept. last. Children born previously not to be illegitimated. Lib. TH #2, Fol. 219. 6 Jan. 1810 [67-1809]

GAINES, Anna Maria. See Anna Maria January.

GAINES, Almira. See Almira January.

GAINES, Henry (Sr. and Jr.). See Henry January.

GAINES, Jerome. See Jerome January.

GAINES, Marion. See Marion January.

GAINES, Sarah Ann, of Baltimore City, divorced from John B. Gaines. 11 Feb. 1848 [64-1847]

GAINES, William. See William January.

GALWAY, Robert, of Baltimore City, divorced from Margaret Galway. 27 Feb. 1850 [292-1849]

GETTIER, Frances. See Frances Smith.

GIBSON, Eliza, of Baltimore City, divorced from Edmund D. Gibson. 9 Mar. 1850 [558-1849]

GIBSON, ELizabeth, of Baltimore City, divorced from John Gibson. She to have custody of children. (See 15-1836.) 20 Feb. 1836 [70-1835]

GIBSON, Elizabeth, of Harford Co., divorced from William Gibson. 17 Feb. 1827 [160-1826]

GIBSON, John Thomas. See John Thomas Wood.

GIBSON, Maria. See Maria Wood.

GIBSON, Mary Ann. See Mary Ann Wood.

GIBSON, Richard G. Makall. See Richard G. Makall Wood.

GIBSON, Samuel Wesley. See Samuel Wesley Wood.

GIBSON, Sarah Susan. See Sarah Susan Wood.

GIBSON, William Henry.   See William Henry Wood.

GILDER, Ann, of Queen Anne's Co., divorced from Henry Gilder. She to have custody of child. 17 Feb. 1827 [162-1826]

GILDER, Ann, of Queen Anne's Co., divorced from Henry Gilder. 10. Feb. 1829 [44-1828]

GILDER, Reuben, of Baltimore (city or co. not stated), divorced from Eliza M. Gilder. 12 Feb. 1836 [100-1835]

GILHAM, Ann, alias Gillam, of Anne Arundel Co., divorced from Thomas Gilham, alias Gillam. 31 Mar. 1841 [11-1841 (sp)]

GILL, Stephen.   See Stephen Cole.

GILLLAM.   See also Gilham.

GILMAN, Judson.   See Judson J. Fogg.

GILMORE, James G.   See James G. Kell.

GILMORE, Sarah, of Baltimore City, marriage to David S. Barnum, annulled. See Sarah Barnum. 18 Feb. 1833 [75-1832]

GIRAUD, Augustus J. T., of Baltimore City, marriage to Mary Ann Giraud, annulled. 10 Feb. 1828 [57-1827]

GIRVIN, James, of Cecil Co., divorced from Ann Girvin. 7 Mar. 1850 [519-1849]

GITTINGS, Richard and Elizabeth Gittings, of Baltimore Co., divorced. 22 Feb. 1831 [156-1830]

GODDARD, John.   See Charles Warfield.

GODDARD, Sarah.   See Charles Warfield.

GODFREY, Sarah, of Baltimore Co., divorced from Henry Godfrey. She to have custody of children. 17 Mar. 1837 [206-1836]

GODMAN, Thomas W., of Baltimore City, divorced from Emeline Godman. 14 Mar. 1834 [247-1833]

GOOD, Jacob. See Mary Gwinn.

GOOD, Mary. See Thomas Boylan.

GOODEN, James, of Prince George's Co., divorced from Jane Gooden. 18 Feb. 1841 [73-1840]

GOODWIN, Charles C., son of William Goodwin, name changed to Charles C. Ridgely. 14 Dec. 1790 [10-1790]

GOODWIN, Charles, son of Lyde Goodwin, name changed to Charles Ridgely. 14 Dec. 1790 [10-1790]

GORDY, Julia Ann, of Worcester Co., divorced from William Quinton Gordy. 9 Feb. 1838 [85-1837]

GORRELL, Thomas, (of Hannah), of Harford Co., a minor, name changed to Thomas Jeffery. 12 Jan. 1825 [19-1824]

GORSUCH, William Henry. See William Henry Shipley.

GOULD, Thomas. See Thomas Nicholson.

GOULEY, Louis H., of Baltimore City, divorced from Mary Gouley. 19 Mar. 1840 [312-1839]

GOWAN, Catharine, divorced from James Gowan. 2 Mar. 1838 [122-1837]

GRACE, Mary, of Baltimore Co., divorced from William C. Grace. 12 Mar. 1840 [249-1839]

GRAHAM, Martha, of Frederick Co., divorced from Augustus Graham. 3 Feb. 1817 [213-1816]

GRANT, Lewis. See Lewis Grant Davidson.

GRATZ, Margaret E., of Baltimore City, divorced from Hyman Gratz, Jr. 31 Jan. 1846 [53-1845]

GRATZ, Margaret E., of Baltimore City, name changed to Margaret E. Martin. 10 Mar. 1846 [343-1845]

GRAY, Ellender, of Anne Arundel Co., divorced from Edward Gray. 5 Feb. 1824 [99-1823]

GREASON, Joanna, of Frederick Co., annullment from William Greason. 27 Mar. 1838 [352-1837]

GREEN, Alice, of Prince George's Co., divorced from Thomas Green. 6 Mar. 1838 [132-1837]

GREENWELL, Lydia Ann, of Annapolis, divorced from Joseph W. Greenwell. 6 Apr. 1841 [58-1841 (sp)]

GRIFFITH, Daniel, of Baltimore City, divorced from Margaret Griffith. 29 Mar. 1838 [288-1837]

GRIFFITH, Margaret, of Baltimore City, divorced from James Griffith. 19 Feb. 1941 [88-1840]

GRIM, Thomas Didymus, of Washington Co., name changed to Thomas Didymus Grey Grim. His acts as Justice of the Peace under former name, confirmed. 5 Mar. 1847 [184-1846]

GRIMES, Mary, married in 1789 or 1790 to Peter
Deal, then living in Frederick Co. The
following summer he abandoned her, and
has not been heard of since. She thought
he was dead. She then married in 1798 to
Basil Grimes, of Frederick Co., by whom
she has nine children. Marriage to
Grimes confirmed and childred declared
legitimate. 6 Mar. 1829 [116-1828]

GRUPY, Francis, of Baltimore Co., divorced
from Sarah B. Grupy. 9 Mar. 1841 [239-
1840]

GUNBY, Theodore, of Somerset Co., name changed
to Theodore Gunby Dashiell. Lib. TH #3,
Fol. 376. 5 Dec. 1812 [41-1812]

GUY, Mary, of St. Mary's Co., name changed to
Mary Morgan. 1 Mar. 1852 [38-1852]

GUYTON, Andrew Jackson, of Washington Co.,
name changed to Andrew Jackson Clingan.
25 Feb. 1829 [133-1828]

GWINN, Mary, of Taneytown, Frederick Co.,
about the year 1791 married Thomas Boylan, then of the same county. She was
siezed of certain real estate, which she
held by devise under will of her father,
Jacob Good. Shortly after marriage she
learned Boylan had another wife living in
Ireland, in consequence Boylan ran away
and she has never heard any certain ac-
count of him since. Several years later
in full confidence that Boylan was married at the time he married her, she
married John Gwinn, by whom she had several children. Children by Gwinn made
legitimate as if Boylan had died or she
had never been married to him. See Thomas Boylan. 20 Jan. 1808 [73-1807]

GWINN, Mary, of Frederick Co., marriage annulled. Her marriage to John Gwinn, now

38

deceased, confirmed. Lib. TH #2, Fol. 9.
20 Dec. 1808 [13-1808]

HALL, Emeline R., of Somerset Co., divorced
from John M. Hall. County Court or Court
of Chancery to set alimony. She to resume maiden name, Adams. 6 Mar. 1834
[161-1833]

HALL, Francis, Jr., of Queen Anne's Co., name
changed to Francis Hall Rozer and he is
given right to bear coat-of-arms and
armorial bearings of the Rozer family.
22 Dec. 1792 [24-1792]

HALL, Levin Wall, name changed to Levin Hall
Wall. 12 Jan. 1831 [3-1830]

HALL, Mary Elizabeth, infant daughter of Levin
Wall Hall, name changed to Elizabeth
Wall. 12 Jan. 1831 [3-1830]

HALL, Mary Louisa, of Baltimore City, divorced
from Francis C. Hall. 6 Feb. 1819 [144-
1818]

HALL, Richard C., of Prince George's Co., and
Mary Hall, marriage annulled and divorced. 8 Mar. 1828 [130-1827]

HALL, Rose Ann, wife of Levin Wall Hall, name
changed to Rose Ann Wall. 12 Jan. 1831
[3-1830]

HALL, Sarah A., of Frederick Co., divorced
from John H. Hall. 29 Mar. 1836 [273-
1835]

HAMILTON, Amelia, authority over her by her
husband, George C. Hamilton, of Washington Co., annulled. 7 Feb. 1825 [107-
1824]

HAMMER, Mary, of Baltimore City, divorced from
James J. Hammer. Children not to be

illegitimated and to retain right of inheritance. 25 Mar. 1836 [190-1835]

HAMMERSLEY, William, of Charles Co., name changed to William Hammersley Pile. His uncle, Henry Pile, of Charles Co., devised to him and desired he change his name to Pile. 28 May 1813 [10-1813 (sp)]

HAMMERSLEY, Francis, son of William, of Charles Co., name changed to Francis Hammersley Pile. See above. 28 May 1813 [10-1813 (sp)]

HAMMOND, Anna Rebecca, of Frederick Co., divorced from Louis (Lewis) Hammond. She not to remarry. 30 Mar. 1839 [284-1838]

HAMMOND, Elizabeth, of Washington Co., control over her by Johnsa Hammond, annulled. 2 Mar. 1826 [153-1825]

HANDY, Sally, of Dorchester Co., divorced from John Handy. 16 Feb. 1821 [193-1820]

HARDIKEN, Elizabeth, of Dorchester Co., divorced from William Hardiken. 13 Feb. 1828 [53-1827]

HARDING, Eliza, of Dorchester Co., divorced from Matthew Harding. 25 Jan. 1838 [22-1837]

HARDING, Elizabeth, of Baltimore City, divorced from William Harding. 5 Feb. 1824 [104-1823]

HARDING, Rachel, of Baltimore City, divorced from John H. Harding. She to have custody of child/children. 12 Feb. 1838 [49-1837]

HARDMAN, Henry. See Margaret Razer.

HARDMAN, Joseph. See Margaret Razer.

HARDMAN. See Margaret Razer.

HARMAN, Ann, divorced from Henry Harman of Cecil Co. She to have custody of children. 23 Mar. 1833 [283-1832]

HARRIS, Henrietta, of Baltimore City, divorced from Gowin Harris. She to have custody of child/children. 21 Mar. 1837 [291-1836]

HARRIS, William, of Talbot Co., divorced from Elizabeth L. Harris. 16 Jan. 1838 [74-1837]

HARRISON, Lewis. See Lewis Cullember.

HARRISON, Nicholas Connelly, divorced from Mary Harrison, of Talbot Co. 12 Mar. 1832 [283-1831]

HARTMAN, Rebecca, of Baltimore City, and Charles Ferdinand Hartman, marriage annulled. She to use name of Rebecca Roach. 15 Mar. 1828 [203-1827]

HARVEY, Joseph, of Baltimore City, divorced from Rebecca C. Harvey. 10 Mar. 1832 [260-1831]

HARWOOD, Lucretia M. See Lucretia M. Watkins.

HATTON, Henrietta. See Henrietta Love.

HATTON, John C. and Elizabeth Hatton, of Somerset Co., marriage annulled and divorced. Children not to be illegitimated. Lib. TH #2, Fol. 28. 20 Dec. 1808 [32-1808]

HAUPTMAN, William, of Baltimore City, name changed to William Hoffman. 9 Mar. 1846 [341-1845]

41

HAWKE, Josephine, of Annapolis, divorced from Richard James Hawke. She not to remarry. 10 Mar. 1841 [243-1840]

HAWKE, Josephine, of Annapolis, was divorced at Dec. 1840 Session, now empowered to resume her maiden name, Josephine Street Elworthy. 30 Mar. 1841 [54-1841 (sp)]

HAWKINS, Henry John. See Henry John Dovelin.

HAYES, John, of Baltimore City, divorced from Harriet Hayes. 16 Mar. 1840 [261-1839]

HAYES, Robert H., of Cecil Co., divorced from Eleanor Hayes. Neither to remarry. See also 183-1833. 5 Mar. 1834 [94-1833]

HAYGHE, Joseph. See Joseph Huyghe.

HAYNE, Ann B. See Ann B. Wilcox.

HAYNE, Grafton. See Ann B. Wilcox.

HAYNE, Wesley B. See Ann B. Wilcox.

HAYES, James, of Baltimore City, divorced from Mary Ann Hays. 11 Mar. 1840 [238-1839]

HEARN, Elizabeth N., of Worcester Co., divorced from James R. Hearn. She to resume her maiden name, Lindsey. 24 Feb. 1842 [244-1841]

HEBB, Thomas, of Caleb, of St. Mary's Co., name changed to Thomas Broome Hebb. 30 Jan. 1839 [31-1838]

HELMKIN, John C., of Baltimore City, divorced from Eliza Helmkin. 15 Mar. 1833 [205-1832]

HENRY, Mary, of Frederick Co., divorced from Charles Henry. 7 Feb. 1818 [140-1817]

HETZELBERGER, Nicholas, of Baltimore City, divorced from Amelia Hetzelberger. 9 Mar. 1826 [227-1825]

HEWITT, Henrietta, of Baltimore City, divorced from William Hewitt. She to have custody of children. 14 Feb. 1827 [86-1826]

HICKS, Margaret, of Baltimore City, divorced from John Hicks. 8 Feb. 1823 [125-1822]

HICKSON, Mary, of Frederick Co., divorced from Henry Hickson. She to have custody of child. 8 Mar. 1832 [269-1831]

HILDEBRANDT, Susanna, of Baltimore City, divorced from Nicholas William G. Hildebrandt, formerly of Hamburg, but now of Baltimore City. She to have custody of their child. 12 Feb. 1848 [80-1847]

HILL, Clement, son of Charles Hill, of Prince George's Co., name changed to Clement Digges Hill. 2 Feb. 1847 [119-1846]

HINES, William and Mary Hines, of Washington Co., marriage annulled and divorced. Lib. TH #2, Fol. 52. 23 Dec. 1808 [55-1808]

HOFFMAN, Ezra, of Frederick Co., divorced from Mary Ann Hoffman. 5 Mar. 1839 [147-1838]

HOFFMAN, William. See William Hauptman.

HOLLIDAY. See also Hollyday.

HOLLIDAY, Clement. See Clement Holliday Waring.

HOLLINGSWORTH, Edward Ireland, name changed to Edward Ireland. 10 Dec. 1816 [97-1816]

HOLLINGSWORTH, Martha A., of Baltimore Co., divorced from Parkin Hollingsworth. She to use name of Martha A. Kelso, and have custody of their daughter. She not to remarry. 22 Feb. 1830 [121-1829]

HOLMES, Susanna, of Baltimore Co., divorced from William S. Holmes. She to have custody of child. 17 Feb. 1831 [107-1830]

HOLLYDAY. See also Holliday.

HOLLYDAY, Marion, infant daughter of William Hollyday and Nancy Ringold Hollyday, his wife, lately deceased, name changed to Nancy Ringold Hollyday. 31 Jan. 1834 [77-1833]

HOLTZMAN, Conrad, late of Frederick Co., marriage to Eve Holtzman, late Derr, of Frederick Co., but now of Washington Co., annulled and divorced. Children not to be illegitimated. 18 Jan. 1815 [57-1814]

HOOKER, Sophia. See Sophia Porter.

HOOPER, Thomas W., and Frances A. Hooper, marriage annulled and divorced. 8 Jan. 1816 [64-1815]

HOPKINS, Ada, name changed to Ada Burke. 17 Feb. 1847 [57-1846]

HOPKINS, Josephine, name changed to Josephine Burke. 17 Feb. 1847 [57-1846]

HOPKINS, Sarah E. F., name changed to Sarah E. F. Burke. 17 Feb. 1847 [57-1846]

HOPPE, Leah, of Carroll Co., divorced from Frederick Hoppe. 16 Mar. 1840 [256-1839]

HOSKYNS, John Henry and Anne Hoskyns, marriage annulled. He has been guilty of forgery and fled the state, leaving her with three children, one a cripple. Children

44

not to be illegitimated. Lib. TH #3,
Fol. 231. 7 Jan. 1812 [181-1811]

HOUSEHOLDER, Leonard, of Washington Co., divorced from Ellen Householder. 12 Mar.
1836 [104-1835]

HOWARD, James Tolley, of Harford Co., name
changed to James Walter Tolley. 1 Jan.
1827 [1-1826]

HOWELL, Eliza, of Washington Co., divorced
from Isaac Howell. She not to remarry
and to have custody of her child. 20
Feb. 1829 [69-1828]

HOYOT, Jane G., of Baltimore City, divorced
from Thomas J. Hoyot. 14 Mar. 1838
[151-1837]

HUBBARD, Francis, illegitimate child of Lewis
Willson, of Caroline Co., name changed to
Willson 28 Feb. 1844 [193-1843]

HUBBARD, Sarah Elmira, illegitimate child of
Lewis Willson, of Caroline Co., name
changed to Sarah Elmira Willson. 28 Feb.
1844 [193-1843]

HUBBELL, Leah W., of Dorchester Co., divorced
from Josiah Hubbell. 27 Jan. 1819 [68-
1818]

HUBBELL, Leah W., of Dorchester Co., divorced
from Josiah Hubbell. (See above.) 12
Mar. 1829 [157-1828]

HUDSON, Temperance, of Kent Co., divorced from
James Hudson. Her name changed to Temperance Newman. 7 Mar. 1828 [125-1827]

HUGHES, Nancy A., of Allegany Co., divorced
from Robert H. Hughes. She to resume her
maiden name, Nancy Ann Unger. 9 Mar.
1841 [245-1840]

HUNT, Ann, of Anne Arundel Co., divorced from Henry Hunt. 28 Mar. 1839 [304-1838]

HUNT, Lewis, of Baltimore Co., name changed to Lewis Cocky Hunt. 23 Feb. 1832 [145-1831]

HURLOCK, Amelia. See Amelia Sears.

HURLOCK, Ann. See Ann Sears.

HURLOCK, James. See Amelia, Ann, Mary and Willis Sears.

HURLOCK, Mary. See Mary Sears.

HURLOCK, Willis. See Willis Sears.

HUTTON, Elizabeth, of Baltimore Co., divorced from Levi Hutton. 14 Feb. 1818 [217-1817]

HUYGHE, Joseph, of Baltimore City, name changed to Joseph Hayghe. 1 Mar. 1845 [138-1844]

HYATT, Maranda, of Montgomery Co., divorced from Lloyd Hyatt. 14 Mar. 1836 [140-1835]

HYALND, Catherine, of Baltimore City, divorced from Benjamin Hyland. 22 Mar. 1836 [176-1835]

HYNSON, Nathaniel, Jr., of Kent Co., name changed to Nathaniel Thornton Hynson. 22 Jan. 1835 [24-1834]

INGRAM, Sarah. See Sarah Boots.

INSLEY, Joyce, of Dorchester Co., had an illegitimate son, George Slacum Insley, who hath lately died without issue . . . 5 Jan. 1805 [15-1804]

IRELAND, Edward. See Edward Ireland Hollingsworth.

IRVINE, Charlotte Cochran. See Charlotte
Cochran.

IRVINE, Henry Cochran. See Henry Cochran.

ISETT, Ann, of Frederick Co., divorced from
John Isett. She to have custody of infant child. 14 Feb. 1825 [108-1824]

ISETT, Ann, of Frederick Co., name changed to
Ann Royer. 10 Jan. 1837 [12-1836]

ISLEY, Matthew, of Baltimore City, divorced
from Eliza Isley. 11 Feb. 1820 [148-
1819]

JACKSON, Thomas. See Thomas Bond.

JACOBS, John, of Frederick Co., divorced from
Christiana Jacobs. 21 Mar. 1838 [196-
1837]

JACOBS, George. See Louisa Decourtres.

JACOBS, Louisa. See Louisa Decourtres.

JACOBS, Martha, of Baltimore City, divorced
from Benjamin Jacobs. 23 Feb. 1829 [77-
1828]

JAMES, James W., alias James Weeks, late of
Baltimore City, marriage to Mary Ann, nee
Button, annulled and they are divorced.
Children not to be illegitimated. 1 Feb.
1815 [120-1814]

JANUARY, Almira, daughter of Henry and Ann
Maria, name changed to Almira Gaines. 24
Feb. 1847 [94-1846]

JANUARY, Ann Maria, wife of Henry January, name changed to Ann Maria Gaines. 24 Feb. 1847 [94-1846]

JANUARY, Henry, name changed to Henry Gaines. 24 Feb. 1847 [94-1846]

JANUARY, Henry, son of Henry and Ann Maria January, name changed to Henry Gaines. 24 Feb. 1847 [94-1846]

JANUARY, Jerome, son of Henry and Ann Maria January, name changed to Jerome Gaines. 24 Feb. 1847 [94-1846]

JANUARY, Marion, child of Henry and Ann Maria January, name changed to Marion Gaines. 24 Feb. 1847 [95-1846]

JANUARY, William, son of Henry and Ann Maria January, name changed to William Gaines. 24 Feb. 1847 [94-1846]

JAY, Elizabeth, of Washington Co., divorced from William Jay. 12 Feb. 1838 [48-1837]

JEFFERIES, Ann, of Baltimore City, divorced from Gravener M. Jefferies. 12 Jan. 1818 [40-1817]

JEFFERY, Thomas. See Thomas Gorrell.

JENKINS, Albert Francis. See Albert Francis Dixon.

JENNINGS, Charles, name changed to Charles Macgill. See Patrick Macgill. Lib. TH #3, Fol. 139 27 Dec. 1811 [91-1811]

JENNINGS, James, name changed to James Macgill. See Patrick Macgill. [91-1811]

JENNINGS, Nicholas, name changed to Nicholas Macgill. See Patrick Macgill. [91-1811]

JENNINGS, Patrick, name changed to Patrick Macgill. See Patrick Macgill. [98-1811]

JENNINGS, Thomas, name changed to Thomas Macgill. See Patrick Macgill. [98-1811]

JENNINGS, William, name changed to William Macgill. See Patrick Macgill. [98-1811]

JOHNSON, Catharine, of Charles Co., name changed to Catharine Bowie. 24 Jan. 1836 [49-1825]

JOHNSON, Hezekiah, of Charles Co., name changed to Hezekiah Bowie. 24 Jan. 1836. [49-1825]

JOHNSON, Horatio, of Howard District (Anne Arundel Co.), divorced from Priscilla Johnson. 28 Feb. 1850 [164-1849]

JOHNSON, James. See James Bromwell.

JOHNSON, James. See James Michael.

JOHNSON, John Edward. See John Edward Bromwell.

JOHNSON, Levin Lake. See James Bromwell.

JOHNSON, Mary Ann. See James Bromwell.

JOHNSON, Thomas. See James Bromwell.

JOHNSON, William Wesley. See James Bromwell.

JOHNSON, Uriah, of Charles Co., name changed to Uriah Bowie. 24 Jan. 1826 [49-1825]

JOHNSON, Zachariah, of Charles Co., name changed to Zachariah Bowie. 24 Jan. 1826 [49-1825]

JONES, Arnold Elsey, of Somerset Co., name changed to Arnold Elsey. 4 Mar. 1844 [246-1843]

JONES, David, and wife, Elizabeth, of Kent Co., marriage declared valid. David was formerly married to Mary Erickson, who has since died. David and Elizabeth were married December, last, ignorant of the law forbidding a man to marry his wife's sister. No date given. [8-1788]

JONES, Levin, of Baltimore City, divorced from Elizabeth Jane Jones. 10 Mar. 1841 [248-1840]

JONES, Margaret, of Baltimore City, divorced from William P. Jones. She to resume her maiden name of Margaret Weems. 17 Mar. 1840 [334-1839]

JONES, Susannah, of Baltimore City, divorced from John Jones. 13 Feb. 1840 [162-1839]

JUDY, Joseph Leonard, of Frederick Co., name changed to Joseph Lorenzo Judy. 30 Jan. 1850 [48-1849]

JUMP, Samuel Busick, name changed to Samuel Jump Busick, in order to inherit from Senah Busick, of Queen Anne's Co. 5 Dec. 1823 [5-1823]

KAMP, Peter, of Baltimore City, divorced from Amelia Kamp. 20 Mar. 1833 [261-1832]

KANN, Theresa, of Baltimore City, divorced from Julius Kann. 10 Mar. 1838 [146-1837]

KEENE, Harriet. See Harriet Woolford.

KEENE, James. See James Woolford.

KEENE, John. See John Woolford.

KEENE, Josiah. See Josiah Woolford.

KEENE, Samuel Raitt. See Samuel Raitt Creighton.

KEENE, Susan. See Susan Woolford.

KEENE, Susan Emily. See Susan Emily Woolford.

KELL, James G., of St. Mary's Co., name changed to James G. Gilmore. 6 Mar. 1843 [240-1842]

KELLY, Charles, infant grandchild of Elijah Williams, of Somerset Co., name changed to Charles Williams. 3 Mar. 1846 [225-1845]

KELLY, Underwood Rencher, infant grandchild of Elijah Williams, of Somerset Co., name changed to Underwood Rencher Williams. 3 Mar. 1846 [225-1845]

KELSO, Martha A. See Martha A. Hollingsworth.

KEMP, John, of Talbot Co., name changed to John Washington Kemp. 4 Mar. 1835 [149-1834]

KEMPTON, William and Matilda Kempton, of Baltimore City, divorced. 27 Feb. 1830 [180-1829]

KENNEDY, Elizabeth, of Baltimore City, divorced from John Kennedy. She to have custody of children she had by Kennedy as well as children of her former marriage. 2 Apr. 1836 [383-1835]

KEPLINGER, Mary, of Baltimore City, marriage to John Keplinger, annulled and divorced. She to have custody of children. 15 Feb. 1832 [120-1831]

KEPLINGER, Samuel, of Baltimore City, divorced from Mary Keplinger. He to have custody of child/children. 5 Jan. 1838 [2-1837]

KERNER, Elizabeth Jane, of Baltimore City, divorced from Henry F. Kerner. 26 Feb. 1839 [88-1838]

KERR, Sarah, of Baltimore City, divorced from George Kerr. 17 Feb. 1825 [118-1824]

KERSHNER, Elizabeth. See Jacob Kershner. [150-1811]

KERSHNER, Gustavus. See Jacob Kershner. [150-1811]

KERSHNER, Hannah Caroline. See Jacob Kershner. [150-1811]

KERSHNER, Jacob. See Jacob Kershner (below). [150-1811]

KERSHNER, Jacob, of Washington Co., acknowledges his children by Mary Rouck, viz., Sarah, Elizabeth, Jacob, Mary, Gustavus, and Hannah Caroline. Children are declared legitimate and shall take the name of Kershner. Lib. TH #3, Fol. 185. 4 Jan. 1812 [150-1811]

KERSHNER, Mary. See Jacob Kershner. [150-1811]

KERSHNER, Sarah. See Jacob Kershner. [150-1811]

KIDD, Francina, divorced from John Taylor Kidd. She not to remarry. 15 Mar. 1834 [252-1833]

KIMBALL, Daniel K., of Baltimore City, divorced from Mary Kimball. 17 Mar. 1840 [270-1839]

KIMMEL, Theodore, of Baltimore City, divorced from Elizabeth Kimmel. 9 Mar. 1827 [185-1826]

KING, Anna Maria, of Somerset Co., name changed to Aurelia Winder King. 4 Mar. 1840 [220-1839]

KING, Rebecca. See Rebecca Wilson.

KIPER, Christina, of Washington Co., marriage to John Kiper, annulled and divorced. 25 Feb. 1825 [173-1824]

KIRBY, Mary Ann, of Baltimore City, divorced from William Kirby. She to have custody of child. She and child to use her maiden name, Parks. 20 Feb. 1833 [95-1832]

KITE, Eliza, of Baltimore City, divorced from Benjamin Kite. Neither to remarry. 9 Mar. 1832 [246-1831]

KLEIN, Samuel. See Samuel Ulery.

KNOCK, Thomas, of Baltimore Co., divorced from Margaret Knock. She delivered of a colored child in Feb. 1820. 19 Feb. 1822 [177-1821]

KNOCK, Thomas and Margaret Knock, of Baltimore Co., divorced. 29 Feb. 1830 (See above.) [175-1829]

KNOTT, Elizabeth, of Dorchester Co., divorced from James Knott. 22 Jan. 1820 [73-1819]

KNOTTS, James H., of Queen Anne's Co., divorced from Catherine Knotts. 15 Mar. 1839 [186-1838]

LAFFEE, Elizabeth, divorced from Lewis Laffee. 30 Mar. 1839 [285-1838]

LANE, Mary. See Mary Quantrill.

LAPOURILLE, Peter, of Baltimore City, divorced from Jane Lapourille. She not to remarry, Court to have power to bind out any child/children of said Jane, without consent of Peter. 18 Feb. 1830 [94-1829]

LEA, Lewis, See Lewis Pinney.

LEA, Isaac. See Lewis Pinney.

LEAGUE, Elizabeth, of Baltimore City, divorced from Nathaniel J. League. 29 Jan. 1818 [92-1817]

LEE, Anna M. D. See Anna M. D. Shields.

LEE, Eleanor Anne. See James Clerk.

LEE, James Clerk. See James Clerk.

LEE, Margaret Russell Clerk. See James Clerk.

LEONARD, William. See William Marshall.

LEWIS, Mary Ann Maria. See Anna Maria Codling.

LEWIS, Mary E., of Baltimore City, divorced from William W. Lewis. 2 Mar. 1836 [116-1835]

LEWIS, Mary E., had been divorced at Dec. Session 1835 (see above). She thought it was a decree vinculo matrimonii, in reality it was a mensa et thoro. Therefore, on 27 May 1840, she married William Robinson Sheffield, by whom she had two children. By this act, she is divorced vinculo matrimonii from her former husband, William R. Lewis, and her marriage to Sheffield is declared valid. 20 Feb. 1850 [256-1849]

LEWIS, Stephen, of Worcester Co., divorced from Betsey Lewis. 6 Feb. 1819 [145-1818]

LIMBERGER, Christianna, of Washington Co., divorced from Joseph Limberger. She to resume her maiden name, Christianna Seabar. 18 Feb. 1842 [111-1841]

LINDEN, Henry St. James. See James Stephen Thompson.

LINDSEY, Elizabeth N. See Elizabeth N. Hearn.

LITTIG, Ann Maria, of Baltimore City, name changed to Ann Maria Littig Shaffer. 13 Jan. 1845 [8-1844]

LITTIG, Catharine Ann, of Baltimore City, name changed to Catharine Ann Littig Shaffer. 13 Jan. 1845 [8-1844]

LITTIG, Frederick, of Baltimore City, name changed to Frederick Littig Shaffer. 13 Jan. 1845 [8-1844]

LITTIG, Frederick, Jr., of Baltimore City, name changed to Frederick Littig Shaffer, Jr. 13 Jan. 1845 [8-1844]

LITTIG, Hannah Ann, of Baltimore City, name changed to Hannah Ann Littig Shaffer. 13 Jan. 1845 [8-1844]

LITTIG, Julia Bates, of Baltimore City, name changed to Julia Bates Littig Shaffer. 13 Jan. 1845 [8-1844]

LITTIG, Louisa Emily, of Baltimore City, name changed to Louisa Emily Littig Shaffer. 13 Jan. 1845 [8-1844]

LITTIG, Rachel, of Baltimore City, name changed to Rachel Littig Shaffer. 13 Jan. 1845 [8-1844]

LITTIG, William Pitt, of Baltimore City, name changed to William Pitt Littig Shaffer. 13 Jan. 1845 [8-1844]

LITTLE, George and Mary Little, marriage annulled and divorced. Children not to be illegitimated. 29 Dec. 1816 [208-1816]

LOCKERMAN, Townly Chase, divorced from Juliana P. Lockerman. 10 Mar. 1846 [353-1845]

LOVE, Henrietta S., of Baltimore City, marriage to William S. Love, annulled. Her name changed to Henrietta S. Hatton. 27 Feb. 1827 [115-1826]

LOVE, James Francis. See James Francis Corkran.

LOVE, Sarah W., of Baltimore City, divorced from Christopher C. Love. She to have custody of child. 11 Mar. 1840 [239-1839]

LOVE, Thomas Henry. See Thomas Henry Corkran.

LOVEDAY, Eliza. See Eliza Stanley.

LOWE, Adelaide V., of Frederick Co., articles of separation from Bradley S. A. Lowe. She to have custody of infant child, Enoch Lewis Lowe. 4 Feb. 1823 [100-1822]

LOWE, Adelaide V., of Frederick Co., divorced from Bradley S. A. Lowe. (See above.) 7 Feb. 1831 [52-1830]

LOWE, Charles. See Charles Perry.

LOWE, William, of John. See Charles Perry.

LOWRY, Ellen. See Ellen Browning.

LOWRY, James Donaldson, of Baltimore City, name changed to James Lowry Donaldson, in order to inherit from his uncle, James Lowry Donaldson, late of the City of London. 7 Jan. 1804 [81-1803]

LUDDEN, Margaret, of Baltimore City, declared a femme sole. Liability of Lemuel Ludden, annulled. 9 Mar. 1826 [225-1825]

LUSBY, Lucinda D., and Thomas R., of Baltimore City, divorced. She to have custody of children. 15 Feb. 1827 [90-1826]

LUTIG, Sally, of Baltimore City, divorced from John C. Lutig. Children not to be illegitimated. 4 Jan. 1807 [80-1806]

LUTTS, John Jackson. See John Jackson Fullmer.

LYFORD, Margaret Mitchell. See Margaret Mitchell Dickehut.

LYNCH, James, of Cecil Co., divorced from Mary Ann Lynch. 22 Jan. 1838 [21-1837]

McCAY, Elizabeth K., of Baltimore City, marriage to Elijah McCay annulled and divorced. Children not to be illegitimated. Lib. TH #2, fol. 53. 23 Dec. 1808 [58-1808]

McCLAN, Elizabeth. See Charlotte Warfield.

McCLAIN, Mary Ann Josephine. See Mary Ann Josephine Strange.

McCOLLESTER, James. See James Cropper.

McCOURT, Arthur, of Baltimore City, divorced from Elizabeth McCourt. 5 Mar. 1839 [161-1838]

McCOY, Sarah Ann, of Washington Co., divorced from George Valentine McCoy. 6 Mar. 1841 [205-1840]

McCULLOCH, Duncan, of Baltimore City, name changed to Duncan Hugh McCulloch. 21 Feb. 1833 [87-1832]

McDANIEL, Mary, of Washington Co., divorced from Richard McDaniel. 25 Feb. 1825 [186-1824]

McDEVITT, William, name changed to William Wilkinson. 29 Jan. 1850 51-1849

McGREGOR, Alaric. See Alaric Magruder.

McGREGOR, Henry. See Henry Magruder.

McGREGOR, Margaret Ellen. See Margaret Ellen Magruder.

McGREGOR, Nathaniel Mortimer. See Nathaniel Mortimer Magruder.

McGREGOR, Roderick. See Roderick Magruder.

McKENZIE, Thomas. See Thomas Dawson.

McKEWEN, Amanda, of Baltimore City, divorced from William McKewen. 19 Feb. 1841 [188-1840]

McKIERNAN, Catharine, of Washington Co., authorized to hold property aside from her husband, Francis McKiernan. 25 Jan. 1821 [78-1820]

McLEAN, William, of Cornelius, of Baltimore City, name changed to William Henry McLean. 1 Apr. 1839 [319-1838]

McMILLAN, John, of Baltimore City, divorced from Mary Ann McMillan. 13 Feb. 1838 [46-1837]

McNABB, John, of Baltimore City, and Henrietta of Harford Co., marriage annulled and divorced. 10 Mar. 1847 [338-1846]

McNALLY, Patrick, of Baltimore City, divorced from Mary McNally. 15 Jan. 1840 [130-1839]

McNELL, John Wesley, Jr. See John Wesley McNelly, Jr.

McNELL, John Wesley, Sr. See John Wesley McNelly, Sr.

McNELLY, John Wesley, Jr., of Baltimore City, name changed to John Wesley McNell, Jr. 10 Mar. 1843 [256-1842]

McNELLY, John Wesley, Sr., of Baltimore City, name changed to John Wesley McNell, Sr. 10 Mar. 1843 [256-1842]

MACCUBIN. See also Macubbin.

MACCUBIN, James, son of Nicholas Maccubin, Sr. and Mary Clare Maccubin (sister of Charles Carroll, late of Annapolis, barrister), by will of said Carroll, to have coat-of-arms and armorial bearings of Carroll family, and his name changed to James Carroll. No date given. [3-1783]

MACCUBIN, Nicholas, Jr., son of Nicholas Maccubin and Mary Clare Maccubin (sister of Charles Carroll, late of Annapolis, barrister), to have coat-of-arms and armorial bearings of Carroll family and his name changed to Nicholas Carroll. No date given. [3-1783]

MACGILL, Charles. See Patrick Macgill.

MACGILL, James. See Patrick Macgill.

MACGILL, Nicholas. See Patrick Macgill.

MACGILL, Patrick. See Patrick Macgill, below.

MACGILL, Patrick, of Anne Arundel Co., had a daughter, Elizabeth, who intermarried with one William Jennings of Anne Arundel Co. Elizabeth has been dead about two years and William has totally abandoned the children, Charles, James, Nicholas,

Patrick and William. The surnames of the children changed to Macgill. Lib. TH #3, fol. 139. 27 Dec. 1811 [91-1811]

MACGILL, William. See Patrick Macgill.

MACUBBIN, Susannah, of Baltimore City, divorced from Moses Macubbin. 17 Feb. 1826 [76-1825]

MADDOX, Amelia, of Baltimore City, divorced from Samuel H. Maddox. She to have custody of children. 26 Feb. 1824 [207-1823]

MADDOX, Francis. See George Yeaman.

MAGRUDER, Alaric, name changed to Alaric McGregor. 12 Feb. 1821 [135-1820]

MAGRUDER, Henderson Williams. See Henderson Magruder Williams.

MAGRUDER, Henderson Williams. See Marcellus Williams.

MAGRUDER, Henry, name changed to Henry McGregor. 12 Feb. 1821 [135-1820]

MAGRUDER, Margaret Ellen, name changed to Margaret Ellen McGregor. 12 Feb. 1821 [135-1820]

MAGRUDER, Nathaniel Mortimer, name changed to Nathaniel Mortimer McGregor. 12 Feb. 1821 [135-1820]

MAGRUDER, Roderick, name changed to Roderick McGregor. 12 Feb. 1821 [135-1820]

MAKER, Catharine, of Washington Co., name changed to Catharine Coudy. James Coudy and Mahala, his wife, to adopt Catharine. 25 Jan. 1848 [29-1847]

MALEY, Andrew, of Allegany Co., name changed
to Andrew Jackson Maley. 8 Jan. 1847
[6-1846]

MANNING, Mary, of Washington Co., married in
1829 to Wesley Manning, who lived with
her for five years and they had three
children, all of whom are living. Some-
time in 1834 Wesley removed to parts
unknown and has not been seen or heard of
since. Her father, Jacob Sager, died
testate in 1837. John Beard, her father's executor, directed to pay over to
Mary, her share of her father's estate.
29 Mar. 1838 [296-1837]

MARRIOTT, Julianna, of Baltimore Co., authority over her by her husband, Jarvis Marriott, annulled. 24 Feb. 1825 [197-1824]

MARSHALL, Britiana, of Dorchester Co., marriage to Thomas Marshall annulled and
divorced. Children not to be illegitimated. Lib. TH #1, fol. 333. 15 Jan.
1808 [30-1807]

MARSHALL, William, name changed to William
Leonard. 16 Jan. 1845 [57-1844]

MARTIN, Elizabeth, of Baltimore City, divorced
from David Martin. 1 Mar. 1830 [225-
1829]

MARTIN, Emma Olivia. See Emma Olivia Everly.

MARTIN, Margaret E. See Margaret E. Gratz.

MARTIN, Sarah, of Baltimore City, divorced
from William Martin. 6 Mar. 1841 [203-
1840]

MASON, Abraham Barnes, in order to comply with
terms of will of Richard Barnes, late of
St. Mary's Co., name changed to Abraham
Barnes. 19 Jan. 1829 [25-1828]

MASSEY, Lucinda, of Baltimore City, divorced from Thomas Massey. 12 Mar. 1840 [245-1839]

MASTERS, Elizabeth, of Allegany Co., divorced from Christian Masters. 1 Jan. 1820 [23-1819]

MATHEWS, Harriet, of Baltimore Co., divorced from Thomas L. Mathews. 16 Feb. 1821 [192-1820]

MATTHEWS, Ann, of Baltimore City, divorced from Thomas Matthews. She to have custody of her two infant daughters. She to resume her maiden name (not stated). 14 Feb. 1831 [92-1830]

MATTHEWS, Robert H. of Somerset Co., divorced from Sarah Matthews. 12 Mar. 1840 [230-1839]

MAXWELL, George W., of Prince George's Co., divorced from Mary Maxwell. 22 Jan. 1838 [17-1837]

MAXWELL, Sophia Ann. See Sophia Ann Robinson.

MAYER, John. See Mary Ebrecht.

MAYER, Mary. See Mary Ebrecht.

MEAD, Thomas, of Calvert Co., divorced from Sophia Mead. 6 Mar. 1838 [130-1837]

MEDFORD, Eliza. See Eliza Trice.

MEDFORD, William. See William Trice.

MEEDS, John, his marriage to Elizabeth Meeds, of Queen Anne's Co., annulled and divorced. Any children not to be illegitimated. 26 Jan. 1815 [85-1814]

MEEKS, Aquilla Napoleon Howard, name changed to Howard Meeks. 11 Feb. 1841 [60-1840]

MEGINNIS, Mary, of Kent Co., partial divorce from Casparus Meginnis. John Crane appointed trustee of Mary to receive payment from Casparus of $300.00 per year etc. She to retain right of inheritance etc. 5 Feb. 1824 [95-1823]

MELVIN, John, of Baltimore City, divorced from Eleanor Melvin. 14 Mar. 1834 [236-1834]

MERRRILL, Rachel Ann, of Baltimore Co., divorced from John A. Merrill. 31 Jan. 1840 [154-1839]

MERRITT, Sarah E. See Sarah E. Morrison.

MERRYMAN, Ann, of Baltimore (City or County not stated), divorced from William Merryman. 19 Feb. 1822 [170-1821]

MERRYMAN, Horatio R., of District of Columbia, divorced from Sarah A. Merryman, of Baltimore City. 23 Feb. 1838 [89-1837]

MEYER, Frederica, of Baltimore City, divorced from George Meyer. 21 Mar. 1838 [197-1837]

MEYER, Mary K., of Anne Arundel Co., divorced from Christian C. Meyer. 24 Dec. 1863 [100-1862]

MEYERS, Aaron. See Aaron Meyers Rothschild.

MICHAEL, James, of Harford Co., name changed to James Johnson. 29 Jan. 1833 [22-1832]

MILES, Elizabeth, of Baltimore City, divorced from Robert Miles. 26 Feb. 1840 [171-1839]

MILFORD, John. See John Mullen.

MILLEMAN, George, divorced from Mary Milleman. 14 Mar. 1834 [233-1833]

63

MILLINGTON, Henry. See Henry Delahay.

MILLINGTON, James. See James Delahay.

MILLINGTON, Robert. See Henry Delahay.

MILLINGTON, Susan. See Henry Delahay.

MILLS, James, a minor, of Dorchester Co., name changed to James Applegarth. 5 Jan. 1827 [4-1826]

MILLS, John, of Anne, of Dorchester Co., name changed to John Crawford, in order to inherit property. 8 Jan. 1803 [49-1802]

MITCHELL, Frances B., of Baltimore City, divorced from John I. Mitchell. 12 Feb. 1823 [138-1822]

MITCHELL, Sarah, of Calvert Co., divorced from Samuel Mitchell. She to resume maiden name of Howes. 13 Feb. 1835 [69-1834]

MITCHELL, Theodore, of Anne Arundel Co., name changed to Theodore Swain. He is natural son of Mary Mitchell, by John Swain. Name confirmed and his marriage made valid. Lib. TH #2, fol. 557. 24 Dec. 1810 [86-1810]

MOBLY, Elizabeth, of Washington Co., divorced from Joseph Mobly. 10 Mar. 1837 [178-1836]

MOORE, Lydia, of Baltimore City, divorced from John Moore. 22 Jan. 1838 [18-1837]

MORGAN, Mary. See Mary Guy.

MORRIS, Henrietta, of Charles Co., divorced from James Morris. She not to remarry. She to have custody of children. 21 Mar. 1835 [297-1834]

MORRIS, John, alias John Morrison. 29 Jan.
1829 [10-1828]

MORRISON, John. See John Morris.

MORRISON, Sarah E., name changed to Sarah E.
Merritt. 1 Mar. 1845 [137-1844]

MOUSLEY, Rachel, of Cecil Co., divorced from
John Mousley. She to take name Rachel
Simpson. 9 Mar. 1850 [503-1849]

MULLEN, John, of Montgomery Co., name changed
to Samuel Milford. 4 June 1836 [375-
1835]

MULLIKEN, Amanda, of Baltimore City, divorced
from Edward P. Mulliken. 2 Mar. 1841
[189-1840]

MURPHY, Noah, of Caroline Co., divorced from
Susan Murphy. 9 Mar. 1850 [560-1849]

MURRAY, John. See Sophia Ann Robinson.

MURRAY, John Staup. See John Staup.

MURRAY, Matthew, carver, of Baltimore City,
name changed to Heron Campbell Murray.
23 Jan. 1847 [25-1846]

MURRAY, William Vans. See William Vans Robertson.

MUSKETT, John. See Archibald Alexander.

MUSKETT, Susanna. See Archibald Alexander.

MYERS, Catharina and Daniel Myers, of Frederick Co., divorced. 6 Feb. 1830 [58-
1829]

MYERS, Catharine. See Margaret Razer.

MYERS, Hannah. See John Echer.

MYERS, Nancy, of Allegany Co., divorced from
    Jacob Myers. 9 Mar. 1841 [220-1840]

NAYLOR, Margaret W., of Charles Co., divorced
    from James Naylor (of George). 11 Feb.
    1820 [147-1819]

NEILSON, Ann, of Baltimore Co., divorced from
    Hugh Neilson. 29 Jan. 1817 [155-1816]

NESBIT, Anne. See Anne Smock.

BESBIT, John. See John Smock.

NESBIT, Mary. See Mary Smock.

NESBIT, Robert. See Robert Smock.

NESS, Elizabeth, of Baltimore City, divorced
    from Samuel Ness. She to have custody of
    children. 18 Mar. 1833 [242-1832]

NEVILLE, Sarah Sophia, of Cecil Co., divorced
    from Thomas Neville. She to have custody
    of child/children. 21 Mar. 1837 [244-
    1836]

NEWMAN, Temperance. See Temperance Hudson.

NICHOLS, Ann, of Queen Anne's Co., control of
    Samuel Nichols, annulled. She to have
    custody of children. 11 Feb. 1826 [67-
    1825]

NICHOLSON, Nathan, of Baltimore Co., has an
    illegitimate son, a minor, George Wash-
    ington Eyers. His name changed to George
    Washington Nicholson. 28 Dec. 1793 [3-
    1793]

NICHOLSON, Thomas, of Baltimore City, name
    changed to Thomas Gould. 12 Jan. 1836
    [6-1835]

NICHOLSON, Thomas. See Charlotte Warfield.

NOBLE, Emilie W., of Baltimore City, divorced from Nathaniel G. Noble. 12 Mar. 1839 [181-1838]

NORRIS, James, Sr., of St. Mary's Co., divorced from Sarah Norris. 8 Feb. 1823 [208-1822]

NORRIS, Madison Smith, of Baltimore Co., name changed to Madison Smith Stansbury. 11 Dec. 1821 [4-1821]

NORTH, Priscilla, of Somerset Co., divorced from Edward North. 15 Feb. 1827 [89-1826]

NUGENT, Mary, of Baltimore City, divorced from Arthur Nugent. 18 Feb. 1842 [112-1841]

NUMSEN, Frederick H., of Baltimore City, divorced from Eliza Ann Numsen. 20 Mar. 1839 [213-1838]

O'BRIEN, Cassandra, of Baltimore City, divorced from Hugh O'Brien. Neither to remarry. 7 Feb. 1833 [39-1832]

O'BRIEN, Lucy, of Montgomery Co., divorced from William O'Brien. 8 Mar. 1837 [126-1836]

OFFLEY, Robert and Sarah, of Queen Anne's Co., marriage annulled and divorced. Children not to be illegitimated. Lib. TH #3, fol. 451. 23 Dec. 1812 [117-1812]

OGLE, Laura. See Laura Ogle Oldham.

OLDHAM, Laura Ogle, of Cecil Co., name changed to Laura Ogle. 4 Feb. 1845 [45-1844]

ONION, Zaccheus. See Zaccheus Barret.

OPPERMAN, George Lewis, of Baltimore City,
    divorced from Ann Opperman. 13 Mar. 1827
    [257-1826]

OSCIUS, Charles, of Allegany Co., divorced
    from Louisa Oscius. 3 Feb. 1840 [156-
    1840]

OTTO, Gustavus, of Baltimore City, divorced
    from Sarah Martha Otto. 10 Mar. 1847
    [277-1846]

PADDISON, William, married first Anne Sher-
    wood, who died. He married second, her
    sister, Sarah. His second marriage con-
    firmed. 22 Dec. 1788 [21-1788]

PAGE, Henry. See John Woodland Crisfield.

PAGETT, David Davis, of Kent Co., name changed
    to David Davis. 31 Jan. 1823 [87-1822]

PAINTER, Samuel, of Baltimore Co., divorced
    from Elizabeth Painter. 15 Feb. 1838
    [57-1837]

PANNEL, Elizabeth. See Elizabeth Barling.

PARKE, Margaret, of Baltimore Co., control
    over her by husband, Davis B. Parke,
    annulled. 24 Feb. 1825 [154-1824]

PARKER, Schoolfield, of Worcester Co., mar-
    riage to Sarah Parker, annulled. Sarah
    convicted of adultery and bearing a mul-
    lato child, condemned to servitude and
    sold. Facts proven by certified copies
    from records of Worcester Co. 26 Dec.
    1794 [3-1794]

PARKS, Abraham and Eleanor, of Baltimore Co.,
    marriage annulled and divorced. Children
    not to be illegitimated. Lib. TH #2,
    fol. 473. 23 Dec. 1810 [45-1810]

PARKS, Mary Ann. See Mary Ann Kirby.

PARRAN, Somerset Young, of Calvert Co., name
changed to Charles Somerset Parran. 11
Mar. 1840 [252-1839]

PARRITT, Rebecca, of Anne Arundel Co., divorced from Thomas Parritt. 25 Jan. 1819
[57-1818]

PATRICK, Mary, of Baltimore City, divorced
from Samuel C. Patrick. 25 Feb. 1830
[139-1829]

PATTERSON, Elizabeth, (Betsey). See Elizabeth
Bonaparte.

PATTERSON, Sarah F., of Baltimore City, divorced from Henry P. Patterson. 1 Mar.
1839 [104-1838]

PATTISON, James I., of Baltimore City, divorced from Eleanor Pattison. Deed of separation. 6 Mar. 1838 [244-1837]

PAXTON, Mary Ann, of Frederick Co., divorced
from Robert Paxton. She to have custody
of children. 18 Mar. 1833 [222-1832]

PEDDICORD, Catharine, of Baltimore City, divorced from Joseph Peddicord. 24 Feb.
1841 [123-1840]

PEREGOY, Louisa H., of Cecil Co., divorced
from Nathan W. Peregoy. She to have
custody of child. 6 Mar. 1847 [193-
1846]

PERRIE, Sophia H., of Prince George's Co.,
divorced from Charles E. Perrie. 9 Mar.
1850 [448-1849]

PERKINS, Edmund, of Kent Co., marriage annulled and divorced from Rebecca Perkins.
29 Jan. 1819 [76-1818]

PERRY, Charles, of Dorchester Co., and his children's names changed to Lowe. He was illegitimate child of Mary Perry who later married William Lowe, of John, his reputed father. His father died 1785. Lib. TH #3, Fol. 108. 27 Dec. 1811 [59-1811]

PERRY, Jeremiah, name changed to Jeremiah Perry Davis. He is the only child of the wife of William Smith Davis, by a former husband. 19 Jan. 1805 [97-1804]

PERRY, Joseph B. See Joseph B. Cahall.

PERRY, William Henry. See William Henry Cahall.

PERSHOUSE, John, of Baltimore City, divorced from Elizabeth Pershouse. 9 Feb. 1842 [84-1841]

PERSONETT, Levering, of Queen Anne's Co., divorced from Rachel Personett. 5 Mar. 1839 [149-1838]

PETERS, Amelia, of Queen Anne's Co., and John Peters, marriage annulled and divorced. Children not to be illegitimated. Lib. TH#2, fol. 164. 6 Jan. 1810 [24-1809]

PIERCE, Hannah C., of Baltimore City, divorced from Alfred Pierce. She to resume her maiden name, Hannah C. Fisher. 10 Mar. 1841 [254-1840]

PIERCY, John, of Baltimore City, divorced from Mary Piercy. 15 Mar. 1839 [189-1838]

PILE, Francis. See Francis Hammersley.

PILE, Henry. See William Hammersley.

PILE, William. See William Hammersley.

PINNEY, Lewis, of Baltimore City, an orphan boy, ae about three years, adopted by Isaac Lea, of Baltimore City. His name changed to Lewis Lea. 29 Jan. 1816 [210-1815]

PITT, Sophia, of Dorchester Co., authority over her by husband, John Pitt, annulled. Date not given, probably Feb. 1825. [104-1824]

PLOWDEN, Edmund, of St. Mary's Co., name changed to Edmund Paul Plowden. 16 Mar. 1833 [217-1832]

POLK, William Winder, of Annapolis, surname changed to Pollock. 9 Mar. 1844 [313-1843]

POLLOCK, William Winder. See William Winder Polk.

PORTER, Benjamin. See Henrietta Ferguson.

PORTER, Sally Ann, of Talbot Co., divorced from James Porter. 24 Mar. 1838 [256-1837]

PORTER, Sophia, of Baltimore Co., and Lewis Porter, marriage annulled and divorced. Her name changed to Sophia Hooker. She to have custody of child/children. 27 Jan. 1827 [92-1826]

POST, Sarah Ann. See Sally Ann Post Fechtig.

POST, Sarah Ann, of Washington Co., daughter of George Fechtig, name changed to Sally Ann Post Fechtig (sic) and the act of 293-1839 repealed. 26 Feb. 1847 [126-1846]

POSTELL, Sarah, of Baltimore City, divorced from George A. Postell. 18 Mar. 1835 [218-1834]

POTEET, James, of Harford Co., divorced from Margaret Poteet. 9 Mar. 1829 [143-1828]

POWELL, Julia A. See Julia A. Stuart.

PRENTIS, William, name changed to William Roberdeau Swift. 31 Dec. 1813 [27-1813]

PRESTON, Ann S. See Ann S. Bull.

PRESTON, Fanny M. See Fannie M. Bull.

PRESTON, Henry. See Henry Bull.

PRESTON, Margaret C., of Washington Co., divorced from William H. Preston. She to resume her maiden name, Margaret C. Swartzalder. 7 Mar. 1848 [211-1847]

PRESTON, Mary E. See Mary E. Bull.

PRICE, Catharine. See George and John Womeldorf.

PRICE, Joseph, of Caroline Co., marriage annulled and divorced from Sarah Price. She has eloped from his bed and board and lives with a black man. 18 Jan. 1821 [59-1820]

PRICE, Sarah, divorced from John Price, of Somerset Co. 1 Mar. 1848 [130-1847]

PRICE, William, of Queen Anne's Co., name changed to William Skinner Price. 4 Mar. 1840 [189-1839]

PRICE, William and Margaret Price, marriage annulled and divorced. Lib. TH #2, fol. 543. 24 Dec. 1810 [75-1810]

PRITCH, John, a minor, of Queen Anne's Co., name changed to John Wilmer Story. 7 Feb. 1834 [29-1833]

PURTLE, Martin Luther, of Dorchester Co., name changed to Martin Luther Wall. 25 Jan. 1844 [39-1843]

QUANTRILL, Mary, of Washington Co., divorced from Jesse D. E. Quantrill. She to resume her maiden name, Mary Lane, and to have custody of child/children. 5 Mar. 1839 [146-1838]

QUANTRILL, William Heyser, son of Thomas, of Washington Co., name changed to Jesse Duncan Elliott Quantrill. 30 Jan. 1821 [98-1820]

RAZER, Margaret, of Fredericktown, her husband, Joseph Razer, left her about fourteen years ago with six small children and she has not heard from him since. In 1794 her brother, Maj. Henry Hardman, died intestate. His estate descended to Joseph Hardman, his brother, Mrs. Crum, wife of William Crum, Catharine Myers, and the petitioner, sisters of Henry Hardman. Margaret Razer declared a femme sole. 8 Jan. 1803 [8-1802]

RECTOR, Mary Ann, of Baltimore City, divorced from George Rector. 15 Mar. 1839 [187-1838]

REDDING, Eliza Ann, of Baltimore City, divorced from James Piper Redding. 26 Feb. 1840 [175-1839]

REED, Mary, of Baltimore City, divorced from James Reed. She is to have custody of children. 8 Mar. 1839 [291-1838]

REEDER, Susanna, of St. Mary's Co., divorced from James Reeder. She to have custody of minor child during his minority. 7 Feb. 1831 [47-1830]

REEVER, Abraham, of Frederick Co., divorced from Catharine Reever. 12 Mar. 1836 [105-1835]

REID, Henrietta, of Frederick Co., divorced from William P. Reid. She to resume her maiden name, Henrietta Fish. She not to remarry. 6 Mar. 1837 [142-1836]

RHODES, Caleb, of Baltimore City, divorced from Fanny Rhodes. 22 Mar. 1836 [175-1835]

RICHARDS, Sarah, of Baltimore City, divorced from Isaiah Richards. 10 Mar. 1837 [168-1836]

RICHTER, David, of Baltimore City, divorced from Mary Ann Richter. 24 Feb. 1841 [171-1840]

RICKETTS, Charles, of Somerset Co., name changed to Charles Evans. 26 Jan. 1838 [14-1837]

RIDGELY, Charles. See Charles Carnan. See also Charles Goodwin, Charles C. Goodwin, and Charles Sterrett.

RIDGELY, Harriet, of Baltimore Co., divorced from Greenbury Ridgely. She to have custody of child/children. 9 Jan. 1837 [7-1836]

RIDGELY, James, of Baltimore City, divorced from Eliza G. Ridgely. 18 Mar. 1840 [292-1839]

RILEY, Mary Ann (no residence given), divorced from Philip Riley. 7 Mar. 1850 [547-1849]

RINGOLD, Catherine. See Catherine Demmitt.

RINGOLD, Elizabeth, of Baltimore City, divorced from Perry Ringold. 15 Mar. 1834 [264-1833]

ROACH. See also Roche.

ROACH, Dorcas A., divorced from John J. Roach. 19 Mar. 1839 [203-1838]

ROACH, Rebecca. See Rebecca Hartman.

ROBERTS, Samuel, of Baltimore City, divorced from Mary Ann Roberts. 9 Mar. 1838 [144-1837]

ROBERTSON, William Vans Murray, of Dorchester Co., name changed to William Vans Murray. 7 Dec. 1821 [1-1821]

ROBINS, Thomas Littleton, of Worcester Co., infant son of James B. Robins, late of Worcester Co., deceased, name changed to James Bowdoin Robins. 6 Jan. 1827 [77-1826]

ROBINSON, Sophia Ann, formerly Sophia Ann Maxwell, of Dorchester Co., is heir under will of John Murray, late of Dorchester Co., deceased. Sophia's husband has been many years absent, without providing support. She is declared a femme sole. 9 Mar. 1846 [332-1845]

ROCHE, Mary Ann, of Baltimore City, divorced from Morris Roche, of Kent Co. She to have custody of children and she and they to use her surname, Yate. 20 Mar. 1835 [257-1834]

RODERIGUEZ, Michael Adalid. See Michael Adalid.

RODGERS, Lucinda, of Allegany Co., divorced from Arthur M. Rodgers. She to have custody of minor child, not to remarry. 5 Mar. 1833 [127-1832]

ROE. See also Wroe.

ROMYN, John H., divorced from Clara W. Romyn. 26 Feb. 1834 [129-1833]

ROTHSCHILD, Aaron Meyers, of Baltimore City, name changed to Aaron Meyers. 5 Mar. 1844 [258-1843]

ROUCK, Peter, of Washington Co., acknowledges his children by Eve Cassell, viz., Elizabeth, Catharine, and Sarah. Children declared legitimate and shall take the name of Rouck. Lib. TH #3, fol. 185. 4 Jan. 1812 [150-1811]

ROUSE, Elmira, of Baltimore City, divorced from Philip Rouse. 1 Mar. 1850 [191-1849]

ROYER, Ann. See Ann Isett.

ROZER, Francis Hall. See Francis Hall, Jr.

RUSSELL, John, and Eleanor, of Charles Co., granted absolute divorce. 25 June 1830 [16-1829]

RUSSELL, Josephine, of Baltimore City, divorced from William H. Russell. 8 Mar. 1848 [216-1847]

RUSSELL, Capt. Theophilas, of Kent Co., divorced from Ann Russell. 13 Jan. 1823 [43-1822]

SAGER, Jacob. See Mary Manning.

SAMSON, George, and Pamela Sampson married in 1801 and had issue now living. He drank which "deranged his mind." Their marriage annulled and they are divorced. Infant child mentioned. 3 Jan. 1807 [34-1806]

SANFORD, Mary Amanda, daughter of Alexander Sandford. See James Bosworth.

SANDMAN, Sarah, of Washington Co., divorced from Jacob Sandman. 12 Mar. 1829 [172-1828]

SANDS, Bethiah, of Baltimore City, divorced from John Sands. She to have custody of children. 22 Mar. 1833 [281-1833]

SATTERFIELD, Sarah, of Caroline Co., divorced from James Satterfield. 10 Mar. 1836 [106-1835]

SCHAPER, Mary, of Baltimore City, divorced from Henry Schaper. 1 Mar. 1842 [159-1841]

SCHWARTZE, Charlotte, of Washington Co., control over her by husband, Francis P. Schwartze, annulled. She to have custody of children during their minority. 28 Jan. 1826 [44-1825]

SCOTT, Otho. See Otho Taylor.

SCOTT, Sarah Ann. See Sarah Ann Stansbury.

SCOTT, William, and Anna Maria Scott, of Baltimore City, divorced. 7 Feb. 1827 [66-1826]

SEABAR, Christianna. See Christianna Limebarger.

SEARS, Amelia, illegitimate daughter of James Hurlock, of Dorchester Co., name changed to Amelia Hurlock. 6 Mar. 1839 [152-1838]

SEARS, Ann, illegitimate daughter of James Hurlock, of Dorchester Co., name changed to Ann Hurlock. 6 Mar. 1839 [152-1838]

SEARS, Mary, illegitimate daughter of James Hurlock, of Dorchester Co., name changed to Mary Hurlock. 6 Mar. 1839 [152-1838]

SEARS, Sarah Ann, of Calvert Co., divorced from Robert Sears. Children not to be illegitimated or deprived of right of inheritance. 8 Feb. 1837 [44-1836]

SEARS, Willis, illegitimate son of James Hurlock, of Dorchester Co., name changed to Willis Hurlock. 6 Mar. 1839 [152-1838]

SEDGEWICK, Christian, name changed to Christian Adreon. 25 Jan. 1805 [5-1805]

SEDGEWICK, George, name changed to George Adreon. 25 Jan. 1805 [5-1805]

SEDGEWICK, Jacob, name changed to Jacob Adreon. 25 Jan. 1805 [5-1805]

SEDGEWICK, Matthias, name changed to Matthias Adreon. 25 Jan. 1805 [5-1805]

SELBY, Eliza, of Baltimore City, divorced from James Selby. She to take and use name of Farrin and not to remarry. 16 Feb. 1833 [60-1832]

SENTEE, William, of Harford Co., name changed to William Carlen, James Carlen having adopted him. 25 Jan. 1806 [30-1805]

SENTZ, Sarah, of Carroll Co., divorced from Andrew Sentz. 3 Apr. 1839 [365-1838]

SEWALL, John, of Talbot Co., marriage to Eve Sewall, annulled. Eve convicted of adultery and of bearing a mullato child. She and child condemned to servitude and sold, as appears by certified copies of records of Talbot Co. Court. 21 Dec. 1790 [25-1790]

SHAEFFER, Maybell, of Washington Co., divorced
    from Joseph Schaeffer. 9 Mar. 1850
    [440-1849]

SHAFFER, Anna Maria Littig. See Anna Maria
    Littig.

SHAFFER, Catherine Ann Littig. See Catherine
    Ann Littig.

SHAFFER, Frederick Littig, Jr. See Frederick
    Littig, Jr.

SHAFFER, Frederick Littig. See Frederick
    Littig.

SHAFFER, Hannah Ann Littig. See Hannah Ann
    Littig.

SHAFFER, Julia Bates Littig. See Julia Bates
    Littig.

SHAFFER, Louisa Emily Littig. See Louisa
    Emily Littig.

SHAFFER, Rachel Littig. See Rachel Littig.

SHAFFER, William Pitt Littig. See William
    Pitt Littig.

SHALLUS, Sarah A., of Baltimore City, divorced
    from Samuel W. Shallus. 18 Feb. 1842
    [114-1841]

SHANKS, John T., of Dorchester Co., divorced
    from Lydia Shanks. 22 Feb. 1826 [106-
    1825]

SHAW, Elizabeth Ellen. See Ellen Ambrouse.

SHAW, Sophia Elizabeth. See Sophia Ann Weare.

SHAYS, Elijah, of Cayuga Co., New York, and
    Rose Shays, of Somerset Co., Maryland,
    marriage annulled and divorced. Children

not illegitimated. Lib. TH #3, fol. 429. 19 Dec. 1812 [87-1812]

SHEFFIELD, Frederick, of Baltimore City, divorced from Celestia Sheffield. 14 Mar. 1834 [237-1833]

SHEFFIELD, Mary E. See Mary E. Lewis.

SHEFFIELD, William Robinson. See Mary E. Lewis. [256-1849]

SHEFFIELD, William R., of Baltimore City, divorced from Mary Elizabeth Sheffield. 21 Mar. 1838 [199-1837]

SHELLMAN, Charlotte, of Frederick Co., divorced from Jacob Shellman. 9 Mar. 1842 [269-1841]

SHERER, Mary Ann, of Frederick Co., divorced from David N. Sherer. She to resume her maiden name, Mary Ann Shyrock. 15 Jan. 1840 [129-1839]

SHERWOOD, Anne. See William Paddison

SHERWOOD, Sarah. See William Paddison

SHIELDS, Anna M. D., of Talbot Co., divorced from John V. Shields. She to resume her maiden name, Anna M. D. Lee. 6 Mar. 1847 [222-1846]

SHIPLEY, William Henry, of Carroll Co., name changed to William Henry Gorsuch. 20 May 1852 [238-1852]

SHOEBROOKS, Elizabeth, of Queen Anne's Co., divorced from James Shoebrooks. 13 Feb. 1829 [45-1828]

SHOPPY, Elizabeth, of Baltimore City, divorced from Simon Shoppy. She to have custody of any issue. 17 Mar. 1835 [216-1834]

SHRIVE, Barbara. See Richard Taylor.

SHRIVE, George. See Richard Taylor.

SHRIVE, Richard. See Richard Taylor.

SHYROCK, Mary Ann. See Mary Ann Sherer.

SICARD, Frances Ida, of Baltimore City, divorced from her husband, Jean A. Sicard. She to take name of Frances Ida Downer. 6 Mar. 1834 [158-1833]

SIGLER, Ann E. B., of Baltimore Co., marriage annulled and divorced from William Sigler. She to use name Ann E. B. Coggeshall. 10 Mar. 1847 [345-1846]

SILRATT, Elizabeth, of Baltimore City, divorced from Henry Silratt. She to have custody of children by her present marriage. 23 Mar. 1836 [187-1835]

SIM, Patrick, and Ariana Sim, marriage annulled and divorced. Children not to be illegitimated. Lib. TH #1, Fol. 316. 18 Jan. 1808 [22-1807]

SIMPSON, Rachel. See Rachel Mousley.

SKILES, Susanna, of Frederick Co., divorced from John C. Skiles. 14 Mar. 1834 [236-1833]

SLYE, Norris, M. J., of St. Mary's Co., name changed to Daniel Webster Slye. 24 Mar. 1836 [192-1835]

SMITH, Caleb, of Dorchester Co., name changed to Caleb Bell. 12 Jan. 1831 [4-1830]

SMITH, Elizabeth, of Washington Co., divorced from George Smith. She to have custody of the children during their minority. 6 Feb. 1827 [60-1826]

81

SMITH, Frances, of Baltimore City, divorced from George Smith. 10 Feb. 1841 [58-1840]

SMITH, Frances, of Baltimore City, name changed to Frances Gettier. 29 Jan. 1850 [35-1849]

SMITH, Frances Carr. See Frances Wakeman Carr.

SMITH, Isaac, of Washington Co., name changed to Isaac Smith Clayton. 21 Jan. 1841 [23-1840]

SMITH, John, of Baltimore City, divorced from Margaret Smith. 5 Mar. 1839 [162-1838]

SMITH, John, of Baltimore City, name changed to John Charles Alexander Smith. 15 Feb. 1846 [50-1846]

SMITH, Mary, of Baltimore City, partial divorce from John Smith. 4 Feb. 1824 [98-1823]

SMITH, Mary, of Baltimore City, divorced from John Smith. 17 Mar. 1840 [271-1839]

SMITH, Ruth, of Frederick Co., divorced from Samuel R. Smith. 31 Mar. 1841 [48-1841 (sp)]

SMITH, William, of Calvert Co., divorced from Sarah Smith. 19 Feb. 1822 [178-1821]

SMOCK, Anne, of Baltimore City, name changed to Anne Nesbit. 31 Dec. 1801 [25-1801]

SMOCK, John, of Baltimore City, name changed to John Nesbit. 31 Dec. 1801 [25-1801]

SMOCK, Mary, of Baltimore City, name changed to Mary Nesbit. 31 Dec. 1801 [25-1801]

SMOCK, Robert, of Baltimore City, name changed to Robert Nesbit. 31 Dec. 1801 [25-1801]

SMOOT, William. See William Connelly.

SNOWDEN, Mary, of Cecil Co., marriage to John Snowden, annulled and divorced. Her name changed to Mary Bailey. She to have custody of children. 13 Feb. 1827 [83-1826]

SNYDER, Elizabeth R., of Baltimore Co., divorced from Charles L. Snyder. 3 Jan. 1818 [34-1817]

SNYDER, William, of Baltimore City, divorced from Louisa Snyder. 5 Feb. 1839 [41-1838]

SNYDER, William, of Carroll Co., name changed to William Bentz. 17 Feb. 1847 [58-1846]

SOLLARS, Hester Ann, of Baltimore City, divorced from James Sollars. She to have custody of child/children. 11 Feb. 1830 [71-1829]

SOLLARS, Thomas, of Anne Arundel Co., divorced from Catharine Sollars. 18 Feb. 1842 [113-1841]

STACKHOUSE, Mary M., of Cecil Co., divorced from John Stackhouse. 19 Mar. 1840 [310-1839]

STANLEY, Charles, of Chester Town, Kent Co., name changed to Carl Ludvig Strandberg. He was born in Stockholm, Sweden. Surnames of his children also changed to Strandberg. See below. 11 Feb. 1828 [40-1828]

STANLEY, Charles, Jr., son of Charles, of Kent
Co., name changed to Charles Strandberg,
Jr. 11 Feb. 1828 [40-1828]

STANLEY, Daniel, son of Charles, of Kent Co.,
name changed to Daniel Strandberg. 11
Feb. 1828 [40-1828]

STANLEY, Eliza, daughter of Charles Stanley,
of Kent Co., is married to _____ Loveday
and has children of her own. 11 Feb.
1828 [40-1828]

STANLEY, Henry, son of Charles Stanley, name
changed to Henry Daniel Strandberg. 11
Feb. 1828 [40-1828]

STANLEY, Maria Charlotte, daughter of Charles
Stanley, name changed to Maria Charlotte
Strandberg. 11 Feb. 1828 [40-1828]

STANSBURY, Charity. See Charity Alderson.

STANSBURY, Madison Smith. See Madison Smith
Norris.

STANSBURY, Sarah Ann, of Baltimore City, divorced from David G. Stansbury. She to
have custody of children. She and children to use her maiden name, Scott. 16
Feb. 1833 [59-1832]

START, William, of Queen Anne's Co., divorced
from Catharine Start. 24 Mar. 1838
[233-1837]

STAUP, John, of Baltimore Co., name changed to
John Staup Murray. 15 Dec. 1824 [2-
1824]

STERETT, Charles, son of John Sterett, name
changed to Charles Ridgely. 14 Dec. 1790
[10-1790]

STERETT. See also Sterrett.

STERN, Mary Ann, of Anne Arundel Co., divorced from Thomas Stern. 27 Jan. 1819 [69-1818]

STERRETT, Elizabeth, of Washington Co., divorced from James Sterrett. 13 Feb. 1818 [175-1817]

STEVENS, Emily Ann, of Queen Anne's Co., divorced from James C. Stevens. 25 Feb. 1837 [103-1836]

STEVENS, James C., of Queen Anne's Co., divorced from Emily Ann Stevens. 8 Mar. 1848 [215-1847]

STEVENS, Julia Ann, of Talbot Co., divorced from Charles R. Stevens. 28 Mar. 1838 [329-1837]

STEVENS, Julia Ann, of Talbot Co., divorced. (See above, 329-1827). She to have custody of children. 30 Mar. 1839 [279-1838]

STEVENS, Margaret A., of Carroll Co., divorced from Clemson Stevens. She to resume her maiden name--not stated. 28 Feb. 1850 [206-1849]

STEWART. See also Stuart.

STEWART, Elizabeth, of Baltimore City, divorced from Joseph Stewart. She not to remarry. 9 Mar. 1832 [229-1831]

STEWART, George F., of Baltimore City, divorced from Henrietta Stewart. 7 Mar. 1842 [274-1841]

STEWART, Henrietta T., of Baltimore City, divorced from James Stewart. 13 Mar. 1832 [293-1831]

STEWART, Mary Elizabeth, of Baltimore City, divorced from William S. Stewart. She not to remarry. 25 Feb. 1832 [144-1832]

STEWART, Susan, of Charles Co., divorced from John W. Stewart. 6 Feb. 1836 [51-1835]

STEWART, William L., divorced from Elizabeth Stewart. 6 Jan. 1825 [8-1824]

STOCKWELL, Frances A., divorced from John Stockwell. (No residence given.) 26 Jan. 1837 [83-1836]

STODDARD, Andrew Jackson, name changed to John Marshall Stoddard. 26 Mar. 1838 [251-1837]

STODDARD, John Sands Fell, a native of Maryland, name changed to John Sands Fell. 10 Feb. 1852 [23-1852]

STODDERT, John Truman. See John Truman Stoddert Bowie.

STONE, Samuel, of Baltimore Co., name changed to Samuel Jefferson Stone. 6 Mar. 1839 [145-1838]

STORY, John Wilmer. See John Pritch.

STOVER, Harriet Lydia, divorced from Solomon Stover. She to have custody of children. Neither to remarry. (No residence given.) 14 Jan. 1841 [101-1840]

STUART. See also Stewart.

STUART, Julia A., of Worcester Co., divorced from John W. Stuart. She to resume her maiden name, Julia A. Powell. 5 Mar. 1842 [209-1841]

STRANDBERG, Carl Ludvig. See Charles Stanley.

STRANDBERG, Charles, Jr. See Charles Stanley, Jr.

STRANDBERG, Charles. See Charles Stanley.

STRANDBERG, Henry Daniel. See Henry Stanley.

STRANDBERG, Maria Charlotte. See Maria Charlotte Stanley.

STRANGE, Mary Ann Josephine, of Washington Co., name changed to Mary Ann Josephine McClain. 16 Jan. 1850 [10-1849]

SUNDERLAND, Benjamin, of Baltimore City, divorced from Mary Sunderland. 26 Feb. 1848 [129-1847]

SWAIN, John. See Theodore Mitchell.

SWAIN, Theodore. See Theodore Mitchell

SWARTZALDER, Margaret C. See Margaret C. Preston.

SWIFT, William Roberdeau. See William Prentis.

SWOPE, Virginia, daughter of Jacob and Eliza Swope, of Washington Co., name changed to Josephine Agnes Swope. 16 Jan. 1846 [1-1845]

TALL, Lufkin, of Dorchester Co., born out of wedlock, his mother being a Tall and his father a Traverse. His name established as Lufkin Tall Traverse. 11 Jan. 1828 [5-1827]

TAYLOR, Augusta M., of Baltimore City, divorced from Marcellus K. Taylor. 2 Feb. 1850 [64-1849]

TAYLOR, Barbara, wife of Richard, name changed to Barbara Shrive. 5 Jan. 1837 [3-1836]

TAYLOR, George, son of Richard, name changed to George Shrive. 5 Jan. 1837 [3-1836]

TAYLOR, Julia Ann, of Annapolis, divorced from John T. Taylor. 4 Mar. 1850 [188-1849]

TAYLOR, Otho, of Harford Co., name changed to Otho Scott. 22 Dec. 1818 [20-1818]

TAYLOR, Richard, born out of wedlock, his mother is since dead and he (since) assumed the name, Shrive. His name changed to Richard Shrive. 5 Jan. 1837 [3-1836]

TAYLOR, Sabina Kimble, of Harford Co., name changed to Sabina Catharine Taylor. 14 Jan. 1848 [18-1847]

TAYLOR, Samuel, of Dorchester Co., divorced from Jane Taylor. 1 Feb. 1821 [112-1820]

TAYLOR, Thomas and Phoebe Taylor, marriage annulled and divorced. Thomas committed adultery. Children born prior to this act not to be illegitimated. Lib. TH #2, fol. 486. 23 Dec. 1810 [52-1810]

TAYLOR, Vincent P., and Elizabeth, divorced. They married about 17 or 18 years ago and had issue, (four children) now living. About 9 years ago Vincent went to sea and has been absent since, although he has been seen in the U.S. since his departure. Elizabeth believes he has, since his departure, married again. She fell heir to a small real estate in Caroline Co. Children not to be illegitimated. Lib. TH #3, fol. 504. 29 Dec. 1812 [168-1812]

TEAS, Susanna, marriage to William Teas annulled. 7 Feb. 1820 [130-1819]

TEATE, Benjamin, of Queen Anne's Co., divorced from Mary Teate. 19 Mar. 1839 [210-1838]

TENNISON, Catharine, of Baltimore City, divorced from Joseph B. Tennison. She to have custody of son, Oliver Tennison. 19 Jan. 1826 [38-1825]

THARP, Nancy, of Queen Anne's Co., divorced from Richard Tharp. 13 Mar. 1835 [196-1834]

THELIN, Guillaume. See William Tufts.

THOMAS, Francis, of Frederick Co., divorced from Sarah C. P. Thomas, formerly a resident of and now residing in Virginia. 14 Feb. 1846 [155-1845]

THOMAS, Richard, of Cecil Co., divorced from Susanna Thomas. 8 Mar. 1848 [218-1847]

THOMAS, Sarah, of Baltimore City, divorced from David Thomas. 5 Apr. 1839 [363-1838]

THOMPSON, Anthony Christopher Columbus Americus Vespucius, of Talbot Co., name changed to Absolom Christopher Columbus Americus Vespucius Thompson. 26 Mar. 1838 [360-1837]

THOMPSON, Fannie K., of Anne Arundel Co., name changed to Eleanora Thompson. 18 Feb. 1852 [28-1852]

THOMPSON, George Charles. See George Charles Townes.

THOMPSON, James Stephen, of St. Mary's Co., name changed to Henry Saint James Linden. 15 Jan. 1831 [67-1830]

THOMPSON, John, of St. Mary's Co., name changed to John Melmoth Thompson. 23 Feb. 1837 [118-1836]

THOMPSON, Margaret B., of Baltimore City, divorced from Henry W. Thompson. 10 Mar. 1848 [267-1847]

THOMPSON, William W. See William W. Williams.

THORNBURG, Elizabeth, of Baltimore City, divorced from Thomas Thornburg. 17 Mar. 1840 [269-1839]

TILESTON, Martha, of Baltimore City, divorced from William Tileston. She to have custody of children, Martha Elizabeth and Sarah Abigail Tileston. 5 Mar. 1842 [210-1841]

TILGHMAN, Robert Cooke. See Robert Cooke.

TILLARD, Richard, name changed to Richard Tillard Estep. 25 Feb. 1852 [10-1852]

TODD, Alexander, of Talbot Co., divorced from Margaret Todd. 28 Feb. 1837 [121-1836]

TODD, Jesse Paten, represented to be child of Benjamin Todd, of Frederick Co. Name of Jesse Paten Todd confirmed to him. 1 Mar. 1854 [79-1854]

TODD, Lucy Ellen, represented to be child of Benjamin Todd, of Frederick Co., name of Lucy Ellen Todd confirmed to her. 1 Mar. 1854 [79-1854]

TODD, Mary Ann, of Harford Co., divorced from John T. Todd. 5 Mar. 1839 [110-1838]

TOLLEY, James Walter. See James Tolley Howard.

TOMPKINS, Ann, and William Tompkins, of Cecil Co., divorced. She to have custody of child. She not to remarry. 23 Mar. 1833 [311-1832]

TOWNES, George Charles, of Baltimore City, name changed to George Charles Thompson, to enable him to become the adopted son of Thomas Thompson, sea captain, of Baltimore City. 13 Feb. 1821 [155-1820]

TOWNSEND, Israel, divorced from Mary Townsend. (No place of residence given.) 12 Mar. 1840 [225-1839]

TRAVERSE, Lufkin Tall. See Lufkin Tall.

TRICE, Eliza, of Caroline Co., name changed to Eliza Medford. 19 Dec. 1822 [17-1822]

TRICE, William, of Caroline Co., name changed to William Medford. 19 Dec. 1822 [17-1822]

TRITT, Elizabeth, of Frederick Co., divorced from Joseph Tritt. 25 Mar. 1839 [229-1838]

TRUNDLE, David, son of John L. Trundle, of Montgomery Co., name changed to David Henry Trundle. 3 Mar. 1827 [152-1826]

TRUNDLE, Hezekiah, son of John L. Trundle, of Montgomery Co., name changed to Hezekiah William Trundle. 3 Mar. 1827 [152-1826]

TUCKER, Charles Carroll, of Baltimore City, name changed to Charles Tucker Carroll. 5 Feb. 1852 [25-1852]

TUFTS, William, of Baltimore City, name changed to Guillaume Thelin. 1 Mar. 1854 [32-1854]

TULL, John, and Beersheba Tull, his wife, having lived apart several years, etc., divorced. She to resume her maiden name (not stated). 20 Mar. 1840 [324-1839]

TUNIS, Charles H., and Harriet Tunis, of Anne Arundel Co., marriage annulled and di-

vorced. Children not to be illegitimated. Lib. TH #2, fol. 52. 23 Dec. 1808
[56-1808]

TURNER, John, and Ann O. Turner, of Talbot
Co., divorced. Children not to be illegitimated. 21 Dec. 1815 [17-1815]

TWILLY, George, and Priscilla Twilly, of Worcester Co., divorced. 23 Mar. 1833
[124-1832]

TYLER, John B., of Baltimore Co., divorced
from Rebecca Tyler. 26 Feb. 1839 [89-
1838]

TYSON, Mary, of Cecil Co., divorced from Joseph Tyson. 2 Mar. 1836 [117-1835]

ULERY, Samuel, of Frederick Co., name changed
to Samuel Klein. 14 Jan. 1819 [40-1818]

UNGER, Nancy Ann. See Nancy A. Hughes.

UPTON, Sirena, of Baltimore City, divorced
from Levi Upton. She not to remarry. 15
Feb. 1838 [56-1837]

UTERMOHLE, August, of Baltimore City, divorced
from Frederick Utermohle. 16 Mar. 1840
[259-1839]

VAINE, John, of Caroline Co., name changed to
John Clinton Cooper. 12 Jan. 1825 [18-
1824]

VAUGHN, Charlotte A., of Baltimore City, divorced from John Vaughn. 30 Jan. 1841
[108-1840]

VICKERS, William W., and Rebecca Vickers, of Dorchester Co., divorced. 22 Feb. 1831 [135-1830]

VISSAGE, Nancy, of Harford Co., control of James Vissage, annulled. She to have custody of child. 28 Jan. 1826 [40-1825]

WALGAMOT, Juliann, of Washington Co., divorced from John Walgamot. She to have custody of the children. 14 Mar. 1828 [194-1827]

WALKER, Ezekiel and Anne Margaret Walker, of Baltimore City, marriage annulled. Children not to be illegitimated. Lib. TH #2, fol. 586. 23 Dec. 1810 [70-1810]

WALKER, John Cradock, minor son of Dr. Thomas C. Walker, name changed to John Cradock. 25 Jan. 1826 [26-1825]

WALKER, Mary, of Worcester Co., marriage to Memucan Walker, annulled and divorced. Children born prior to this act not to be illegitimated. Lib. TH #2, fol. 373. 6 Jan. 1810 [156-1809]

WALKER, Thomas Cradock, minor son of Dr. Thomas C. Walker, name changed to Thomas Cradock. 25 Jan. 1826 [26-1825]

WALL, Elizabeth. See Elizabeth Hall.

WALL, Levin. See Levin Wall Hall.

WALL, Martin Luther. See Martin Luther Purtle.

WALL, Rose Ann. See Rose Ann Hall.

WALTER, Jacob, of Allegany Co., divorced from Mary Walter. 17 Mar. 1835 [215-1834]

WALTERS, William, of Baltimore City, divorced from Ann Walters. 1 Mar. 1833 [104-1832]

WARD, Allen, of Baltimore Co., divorced from Harriet Ward. 17 Feb. 1824 [119-1824]

WARD, Cordelia L., divorced from Richard Chauncey Ward. Her name will be Cordelia L. Wright and names of her children Rosell Ward and Anna Ward, shall be Wright. She to have custody of children. 10 Mar. 1848 [269-1847]

WARD, John, of Harford Co., name changed to John Smith Ward. 23 Feb. 1825 [136-1824]

WARD, Thomas F., of St. Mary's Co., divorced from Ann Ward. 22 Jan. 1820 [79-1819]

WARD, Thomas F., of St. Mary's Co., divorced from Ann Ward. 13 Mar. 1832 [278-1831]

WARE, Hamutal, of Baltimore Co., divorced from Thomas Ware. 5 Mar. 1842 [211-1841]

WAREHAM, Sarah, of Washington Co., divorced from William Wareham. She not to remarry. 23 Mar. 1839 [224-1838]

WARFIELD, Allen, of Anne Arundel Co., divorced from Mary Warfield. 2 Mar. 1833 [106-1832]

WARFIELD, Charles, and Sarah Warfield, formerly Sarah Goddard, of Baltimore City, divorced. They lived apart for nearly two years. Articles of Separation dated on or about 25 Jan. 1826, he to make settlement, etc. Charles has conveyed to John Goddard, in trust for Sarah, during her life, a house on the south side of Baltimore Street, in Baltimore City. 16 Feb. 1826 [186-1825]

WARFIELD, Charlotte, of Montgomery Co., married 17 Oct. 1820, to Thomas Nicholson, who was already married. Depositions to be taken concerning marriage of Nicholson to Elizabeth McClan prior to the above date. 12 Feb. 1821 [140-1820]

WARFORD, Richard Colvin, of Baltimore City, name changed to Richard Colvin. 1 Mar. 1854 [22-1854]

WARING, Clement Holliday, name changed to Clement Holliday. 3 Jan. 1800 [77-1799]

WARNER, Thomas, and Ruth Warner, of Baltimore City, marriage annulled. Children not to be illegitimated. Lib. TH #2, fol. 374. 6 Jan. 1810 [159-1809]

WATCHER, John, of Frederick Co., divorced from Sophia Watcher. 6 Mar. 1833 [138-1832]

WATERS, Anna Maria. See Anna Maria Belmear.

WATKINS, Lucretia M., of Anne Arundel Co., control of Richard G. Watkins, annulled. She to use name of Lucretia M. Harwood. 7 Feb. 1827 [63-1826]

WEARE, Sophia Ann, of Washington Co., name changed to Sophia Elizabeth Shaw. 15 Mar. 1834 [269-1833]

WEBB, Ricksom, of Dorchester Co., free colored person, his correct name, rather than Richard Webb. (See 287-1834). 23 Mar. 1836 [261-1835]

WEBSTER, Mildred B., of Prince George's Co., divorced from Zachariah Webster. 12 Feb. 1836 [97-1835]

WEEKS, James. See James W. James.

WEEMS, Margaret. See Margaret Jones.

WESTON, James, of Talbot Co., divorced from Ann J. Weston. 22 Mar. 1838 [269-1837]

WHITE, Alice Fowler, infant daughter of Edward H. White, of Worcester Co., name changed to Alice Priscilla White. 16 Jan. 1845 [11-1845]

WHITE, David H., and Ann White, of Baltimore City, divorced. She to have custody of children. 7 Mar. 1826 [197-1825]

WHITE, Elizabeth Ann, of Baltimore City, divorced from Bennet A. White. 14 Mar. 1838 [152-1837]

WHITE, Henry, of Somerset Co., divorced from Esther White. 9 Feb. 1842 [83-1841]

WHITE, Jerome Boss. See Jerome Boss.

WHITE, Margaretta, of Baltimore City, divorced from William White. 24 Feb. 1841 [170-1840]

WHITE, Richard. See Richard Whiteway.

WHITE, Thomas, of Baltimore City, divorced from Lucinda White. 24 Mar. 1836 [178-1835]

WHITEHILL, Mary, of Frederick Co., control of John Whitehill, annulled. She to have custody of children. 9 Mar. 1826 [212-1825]

WHITELOCK, Margaret, of Baltimore City, divorced from William Whitelock. 5 Mar. 1842 [212-1841]

WHITELY, Rebecca, of Queen Anne's Co., control over her by her husband John Whitely, annulled. 24 Feb. 1825 [161-1824]

WHITEWAY, Richard, of Baltimore City, name changed to Richard White. 18 Jan. 1848 [22-1847]

WILCOX, Ann B., of Baltimore Cit5y, divorced from James Wilcox, of Kent Co. She and her children, Grafton Hayne Wilcox and Wesley B. Wilcox, names changed to Hayne. 21 Mar. 1835 [283-1834]

WILKINSON, George. See Aquila G. Bowen.

WILKINSON, Octavius. See Aquila G. Bowen.

WILKINSON, Rebecca. See Aquila G. Bowen.

WILKINSON, William. See William McDevitt.

WILL, Catherine, of Frederick Co., divorced from George Will. She to have custody of children by her present marriage. 13 Jan. 1827 [13-1826]

WILLHIDE, Mary Elizabeth, a minor, of Frederick Co., name changed to Mary Elizabeth Beam. 1 Apr. 1853 [75-1853]

WILLIAMS, Ann, wife of John. See John Cullember.

WILLIAMS, Ann and James, of Baltimore City, marriage annulled and divorced. 14 Feb. 1825 [103-1824]

WILLIAMS, Charles. See Charles Kelly.

WILLIAMS, Elijah. See Charles Kelly and Underwood Rencher Kelly.

WILLIAMS, Elizabeth, of Worcester Co., divorced from Thomas N. Williams. She to have custody of child. 29 Mar. 1838 [322-1827]

WILLIAMS, Henderson Magruder, name changed to
    Henderson Williams Magruder.   24 Feb.
    1830 [135-1829]

WILLIAMS, John.   See John Cullember.

WILLIAMS, Marcellus, of Prince George's Co.,
    name changed to Henderson Williams Magru-
    der. 1 Mar. 1843 [159-1842]

WILLIAMS, Mary Ann.   See Mary Ann Cullember.

WILLIAMS, Underwood Rencher.   See Underwood
    Rencher Kelly.

WILLIAMS, Virginia, divorced from Isaac Wil-
    liams.   Had been living apart 7 years.
    She to resume her maiden name, (not stat-
    ed).   Children not to be illegitimated.
    18 Mar. 1835 [239-1834]

WILLIAMS, William W., of Dorchester Co., name
    changed to William W. Thompson. 16 Jan.
    1830 [5-1829]

WILLS, Mary, of Dorchester Co., divorced from
    David C. Wills. She to have custody of
    children. 15 Mar. 1839 [185-1838]

WILLSON.   See also Wilson.

WILLSON, Francis. See Francis Hubbard.

WILLSON, Lewis.   See Francis Hubbard and Sarah
    Elmira Hubbard.

WILLSON, Mary, of Baltimore City, divorced
    from John Willson. She to have custody
    of the children. 14 Mar. 1832 [326-
    1831]

WILLSON, Sarah Elmira.   See Sarah Elmira Hub-
    bard.

WILSON, Hannah, of Baltimore Co., divorced from Matthew Wilson. 3 Feb. 1819 [113-1818]

WILSON, Julia Ann, of Dorchester Co., divorced from James Wilson. 12 Mar. 1840 [226-1839]

WILSON, Rebecca, of Montgomery Co., divorced from James Wilson. She to resume her maiden name, Rebecca King. 1 Mar. 1830 [229-1829]

WILSON, Rebecca, divorced from James Wilson, (see above). She to resume her maiden name, Rebecca Fling (sic). 7 Feb. 1831 [57-1830]

WILSON, William Vance. See William V. Wroten.

WINN, Elisha and Mary Winn, of Baltimore City, divorced. 28 Feb. 1826 [98-1825]

WOLFE, Harriet, of Baltimore City, divorced from Thomas Jefferson Wolfe. 8 Mar. 1847 [303-1846]

WOMELDORF, George, of Washington Co., divorced from Catharine Womeldorf, alias Catharine Price. 22 Feb. 1822 [198-1821]

WOMELDORF, John (see above), was mistakenly called George. Error rectified. 3 Jan. 1823 [32-1822]

WOOD, John Thomas, of Calvert Co., name changed to John Thomas Gibson. 3 Mar. 1846 [194-1845]

WOOD, Maria, of Calvert Co., name changed to Maria Gibson. 3 Mar. 1846 [194-1845]

WOOD, Mary Ann, of Calvert Co., name changed to Mary Ann Gibson. 3 Mar. 1846 [194-1845]

WOOD, Richard G. Mackall, name changed to Richard G. Mackall Gibson. 3 Mar. 1846 [194-1845]

WOOD, Samuel Wesley, of Calvert Co., name changed to Samuel Wesley Gibson. 3 Mar. 1846 [194-1845]

WOOD, Sarah Susan, of Calvert Co., name changed to Sarah Susan Gibson. 3 Mar. 1846 [194-1845]

WOOD, William Henry, of Calvert Co., name changed to William Henry Gibson. 3 Mar. 1846 [194-1845]

WOODS, Mary, of Frederick Co., divorced from Michael Woods. 11 Mar. 1837 [170-1836]

WOODWARD, Harriet, of Anne Arundel Co., name changed to Harriet Claggett. 13 Feb. 1821 [156-1820]

WOODWARD, James, of Anne Arundel Co., name changed to James Claggett. 13 Feb. 1821 [156-1820]

WOOLFORD, Harriet, daughter of John and Susan Woolford, of Dorchester Co., name changed to Harriet Keene. 4 Mar. 1841 [193-1840]

WOOLFORD, James, son of John and Susan Woolford, of Dorchester Co., name changed to James Keene. 4 Mar. 1841 [193-1840]

WOOLFORD, John, of Dorchester Co., name changed to John Keene. 4 Mar. 1841 [193-1840]

WOOLFORD, Josiah, son of John and Susan Woolford, of Dorchester Co., name changed to Josiah Keene. 4 Mar. 1841 [193-1840]

WOOLFORD, Susan, wife of John Woolford, name changed to Susan Keene. 4 Mar. 1841 [193-1840]

WOOLFORD, Susan Emily, daughter of John and Susan Woolford, of Dorchester Co., name changed to Susan Emily Keene. 4 Mar. 1841 [193-1840]

WOOTERS, Juliana, of Queen Anne's Co., name changed to Juliana Chambers. 14 Feb. 1843 [71-1842]

WORKMAN, John, of Allegany Co., divorced from Sarah Workman. 4 Mar. 1850 [327-1849]

WORTHINGTON, William Thomas Henry. See William Lemuel Bateman.

WRIGHT, Anna. See Cordelia L. Ward.

WRIGHT, Cordelia L. See Cordelia L. Ward.

WRIGHT, Jane E., of Queen Anne's Co., divorced from Samuel J. Wright. 8 Mar. 1850 [428-1849]

WRIGHT, Rosell. See Cordelia L. Ward.

WROE, Everitt and Mary Wroe, marriage annulled and divorced. 15 Jan. 1814 [68-1813]

WROTEN, William V., of Dorchester Co., name changed to William Vance Wilson. 4 Mar. 1844 [243-1843]

YATE, Mary Ann. See Mary Ann Roche.

YEAMAN, George, of Baltimore City, divorced from his wife, Frances Maddox. 27 Jan. 1823 [79-1822]

YEAMANS, John, of Cecil Co., divorced from Sarah Yeamans. 8 Feb. 1823 [136-1822]

YEAMANS, John and Sarah Yeamans, of Cecil Co., marriage annulled and divorced. 2 Mar. 1827 [139-1826]

YOUNG, Andrew, of Baltimore City, divorced from Maria Young. 6 Feb. 1836 [45-1835]

NAMES CHANGED IN MARYLAND 1855-1867*

A Supplement to
*Divorces and Names Changed in Maryland
by act of the Legislature, 1634-1854*

The original intent at the time of the publication of this book, *Divorces and Names Changed in Maryland 1634-1854*, was to include only divorces. As the work progressed it became apparent that many females in the process of divorce asked and were granted the privilege of resuming their maiden names. So it seemed expedient to include all changes of names.

By 1854, jurisdiction in divorce cases in the state had been ceded to the Chancellor and county courts as Courts of Equity. At this point, the original purpose of the work was accomplished so the work ceased and the book was duly published.

A recent review of the *Laws of Maryland* revealed that an act (311:1868) was passed 30 March 1868, effective immediately, vesting jurisdiction in the matter of changes of name to be granted upon application in the Court, accompanied by a statement of the reason for the request.

It seemed appropriate, therefore, to search out the changes of names by an act of the Legislature from 1855 through 1867 and make them available to researchers. In the following compilation the figures at the end of each entry denote first the chapter and second the session of the legislature in which the act was passed. The abbreviation sp., appearing in parenthesis following these numbers, indicates a special session of the legislature.

BAKER, John Wesley. See John Wesley Pitcock.

BEACH, Fanny Hyde, name changed to Fanny Tabb Brewer. 15 Mar. 1867 [275-1867]

BEHRENS, Maria, of Baltimore City, name changed to Henrietta John. 13 Mar. 1865 [103-1865]

BLOWMEROUR, Anna Elizabeth, of Washington County, name changed to Anna Elizabeth Durnbaugh. 5 Mar. 1860 [275-1860]

BOSLEY, Daniel Orrick, name changed to Daniel Orrick, Jr. 20 Jan. 1860 [53-1860]

BOSLEY, Lucretia. See Lucretia Smithson.

BOWARD, William Perry. See William Perry Brinning.

BOWIE, Robert William, infant son of Bettie Bowie, of Charles County, name changed to William Truman Stoddert. 9 Feb. 1864 [20-1864]

BREWER, Fanny Tabb. See Fanny Hyde Beach.

BRINNING, William Perry, of Hagerstown, Washington County, name changed to William Perry Boward. 23 Jan. 1862 [55-1861 (sp)]

BRITTINGHAM, May, of Somerset Co., name changed to Mary Sterling. 4 Feb. 1862 [27-1861 (sp)]

BROOKBANK, William Columbus, of Charles County, name changed to William Columbus Jones. 4 Feb. 1862 [26-1861 (sp)]

BROWN, William M. Risteau, a native of State of Maryland, name changed to William M. Risteau. 10 Mar. 1864 [400-1864]

BRUNDIGE, John Toy, son of Thomas V. Brundige, of Baltimore City, name changed to John Toy Brundige Worthington. 11 Feb. 1864 [78-1864]

CAHILL, Frederick Jerome. See Frederick Jerome Ridgaway.

CARY, Thomas Holloway, of Worcester County, name changed to Thomas Holloway. 9 Feb. 1864 [24-1864]

CLAGETT, Samuel Albert, of Anne Arundel County, name changed to Albert Clagett. 23 Feb. 1858 [65-1858]

CLARKE, Talbot, infant son of Mrs. Virginia Clarke by her late husband, George A. Clarke, deceased, formerly of Cumberland County, name changed to his father's name to wit, George Augustus Clarke. 11 Feb. 1858 [22-1858]

CLEMENTS, Edward Marion. See Edward Marion Dent.

COX, Samuel. See Samuel Robertson.

DANSKIN, Washington A., Jr. See Washington A. D. Ridgway.

DENT, Edward Marion, of Prince George's County, name changed to Edward Marion Clements. 27 Feb. 1856 [22-1856]

DODSON, Richard, of Baltimore City, name changed to Richard Stearns Dodson. 7 Mar. 1867 [109-1867]

DURNBAUGH, Anna Elizabeth. See Anna Elizabeth Blowmerour.

DUROCHER, Charles Louis. See Charles Louis Durocher McLaughlin.

EDES, Benjamin Long. See Benjamin Edes Long.

EARHART, William Henry. See William Henry Hutton.

EATON, Fannie Honora. See Mary Hicks.

FOWK, William Augustus. See Augustus Fowk Robertson.

FUNK, William Clarke, an orphan minor, of Washington County, name changed to George Smith. 7 Mar. 1862 [195-1861]

GETZENDANNER, Otta Glenn, infant son of Doctor Joseph T. Getzendanner, of Allegany County, name changed to Oscar Glenn Getzendanner. 12 Jan. 1860 [40-1860]

GOVER, William Edwin Plummer. See William Edward Plummer Ward.

GREENHAWK, Rufus Henry, of Talbot County, name changed to Rufus Henry Lowe. 7 Feb. 1866 [160-1866]

HAMILTON, Samuel. See Samuel Hamilton Wright.

HANSON, John David. See Jacob Morris.

HENRY, Albert. See Albert Williams.

HENRY, Charles Edward. See Charles Edward Williams.

HENRY, John Wesley. See John Wesley Williams.

HESSLER, Elizabeth, of Baltimore City, name changed to Elizabeth Schneider. 10 Mar. 1864 [358-1864]

HICKS, Mary, of Caroline County, name changed to Fannie Honora Eaton. 8 Mar. 1865 [37-1865]

HOLLOWAY, Thomas. See Thomas Holloway Cary.

HOOFMAN, Francis, of Woodensburg, Baltimore County, name changed to Francis Hoofman Pelzer. 4 Feb. 1862 [32-1861 (sp)]

HUTTON, William Henry, of Washington County, name changed to William Henry Earhart. 24 Feb. 1860 [79-1860]

HYDE, Samuel Edwin Ridout, of Anne Arundel County, name changed to Samuel Ridout Hyde. 22 Jan. 1862 [60-1861 (sp)]

JOHN, Henrietta. See Maria Behrens.

JOHNSON, Alfred, a native of the State of Maryland, and resident therein, name changed to William Fell Johnson. 11 Feb. 1864 [95-1864]

JONES, Mary, of Prince George's County, name changed to Mary Tuck Jones. 8 Mar. 1860 [344-1860]

JONES, William Columbus. See William Columbus Brookbank.

LEVERING, Robert. See Robert McEldowney.

LEWIS, Mary Elizabeth, of Baltimore City, name changed to Mary Elizabeth Young. 18 Mar. 1867 [242-1867]

LONG, Benjamin Edes, of Baltimore, name changed to Benjamin Long Edes. 12 Feb. 1867 [49-1867]

LONG, Sydney Wilson, son of Sydney C. and Mary Long, of Somerset County, name changed to Sydney Chaille Long. 24 Feb. 1862 [102-1861 (sp)]

LOWE, Rufus Henry. See Rufus Henry Greenhawk.

McCOMAS, David. See David Mertzs.

McELDOWNEY, Robert, of Baltimore City, name changed to Robert Levering. 24 Mar. 1865 [158-1865]

McLAUGHLIN, Charles Louis Durocher, infant son of Dr. David Barnum McLaughlin and Maria Louisa McLaughlin, his wife, name changed to Charles Louis Durocher. 7 Jan. 1862 [25-1861 (sp)]

MAXFIELD, John W. See John White.

MERTZS, David, of Baltimore County, name changed to David Henry McComas. 7 Mar. 1864 [276-1864]

MORRIS, Jacob, of Charles County, name changed to John David Hanson. 28 Jan. 1858 [29-1858]

NEWMAN, Shalmanezer, name changed to Sidney Charles Newman. 9 Mar. 1860 [262-1860]

OLDSON, W. H. C., of Queen Anne's County, name changed to Harry Oldson Palmer. 8 Feb. 1867 [26-1867]

ORRICK, Daniel, Jr. See Daniel Orrick Bosley.

PALMER, Doctor Andrew Dunlap, of Baltimore City, name changed to Andrew Johnson Palmer. 15 Mar. 1867 [274-1867]

PALMER, Harry Oldson. See W. H. C. Oldson.

PARKER, Fannie, of Baltimore City, name changed to Fannie Parker Roelky. 8 Mar. 1865 [38-1865]

PELZER, Francis Hoofman. See Francis Hoofman.

PITCOCK, John Wesley, of Baltimore City, name changed to John Wesley Baker. 11 Jan. 1867 [12-1867]

POWELL, John S. See John S. Smith.

PURNELL, Ellenor Kate, minor daughter of John R. Purnell, of Worcester County, name changed to Emma Catharine Purnell. 17 Jan. 1867 [19-1867]

RIDER, Mary Emeline, minor daughter of William P. Rider, of Somerset County, name changed to Mary Wallace Rider. 27 Feb. 1856 [42-1856]

RIDGAWAY, Frederick Jerome, an infant, of Baltimore City, name changed to Frederick Jerome Cahill. 7 Mar. 1862 [275-1856]

RIDGWAY, Washington A. D., of Baltimore City, name changed to Washington A. Danskin, Jr. 10 Mar. 1856 [275-1856]

RISTEAU, William M. See William A. Risteau Brown.

ROBERTSON, Augustus Fowk, of Charles County, name changed to William Augustus Fowk. 4 Mar. 1864 [291-1864]

ROBERTSON, Samuel, of Charles County, name changed to Samuel Cox. 11 Feb. 1864 [65-1864]

ROELKY, Fannie Parker. See Fannie Parker.

SANDS, Charles, of Baltimore City, name changed to Carlos Sales. 27 Jan. 1865 [4-1865]

SALES, Carlos. See Charles Sands.

SCHILLING, Reverend John, of Allegany County, name changed to John Griffith Schilling. 13 Mar. 1865 [95-1865]

SCHLEY, Henry, of the city of Baltimore, name changed to Benjamin Henry Schley. 27 Feb. 1856 [38-1856]

SCHNEIDER, Elizabeth. See Elizabeth Hessler.

SIMMONS, Zachariah Origen, of Frederick County, name changed to John Simmons. 8 Mar. 1865 [40-1865]

SMITH, George. See William Clarke Funk.

SMITH, George, an orphan minor, of Washington County, name changed to William Clarke Funk. 27 Feb. 1856 [13-1856]

SMITH, John S., of Somerset County, son of Rebecca J. Smith, name changed to John S. Powell. 13 Mar. 1867 [245-1867]

SMITHSON, Lucretia, of Baltimore County, name changed to Lucretia Bosley. 18 Jan. 1860 [34-1860]

STACK, John Francis, of Caroline County, name changed to John Rumbold Stack. 15 Mar. 1867 [311-1867]

STERLING, Mary. See Mary Brittingham.

STODDERT, William Truman. See Robert William Bowie.

STOVER, Luther William, of Carroll County, name changed to Luther William Wiond. 4 Feb. 1864 [7-1864]

WARD, William Edwin Plummer, of Anne Arundel County, name changed to William Edwin Plummer Gover. 7 Mar. 1862 [172-1861 (sp)]

WELSH, Elizabeth. See Elizabeth Wilson.

WELSH, Martha. See Martha Wilson.

WELSH, Oliver Jackson. See Oliver Jackson Wilson.

WELSH, Philemon Henry. See Philemon Henry Wilson.

WELSH, Sarah Lowery. See Sarah Lowery Wilson.

WHITE, John, of the City of Baltimore, name changed to John W. Maxfield. 27 Feb. 1856 [31-1856]

WILLIAMS, Charles Edward, illegitimate child of Isaac Henry and Elizabeth Williams, of Dorchester County, name changed to Charles Edward Henry and he is declared capable of inheriting from his father as if he had been born in lawful wedlock. 9 Mar. 1860 [235-1860]

WILLIAMS, John Wesley, illegitimate son of Issac Henry and Elizabeth Williams, of Dorchester County, name changed to John Wesley Henry and he is declared capable of inheriting from his father as if he were born in lawful wedlock. 9 Mar. 1860 [235-1860]

WILLIAMS, William Albert, illegitimate son of Isaac Henry and Elizabeth Williams, of Dorchester County, name changed to William Albert Henry and he is declared capable of inheriting from his father as if he had been born in lawful wedlock. 9 Mar. 1860 [235-1860]

WILSON, Elizabeth, of Carroll County, name changed to Elizabeth Welsh. 10 Mar. 1856 [217-1856]

WILSON, Martha, of Carroll County, name changed to Martha Welsh. 10 Mar. 1856 [217-1856]

WILSON, Oliver Jackson, of Carroll County, name changed to Oliver Jackson Welsh. 10 Mar. 1856 [217-1856]

WILSON, Philemon Henry, of Carroll County, name changed to Philemon Henry Welsh. 10 Mar. 1856 [217-1856]

WIOND, Luther William.   See William Luther Stover.

WORTHINGTON, John Toy Brundige.   See John Toy Brundeige.

WRIGHT, Samuel Hamilton, of Prince George's County, name changed to Samuel Hamilton. 6 Mar. 1856 [106-1856]

WRIGHT, Thomas Pratt, son of Joseph and Sarah P. Wright, of Somerset County, name changed to Thomas Hicks Wright. 13 Feb. 1862 [133-1861 (sp)]

YOUNG, John, of Baltimore City, name changed to John Marshall Young. 8 Feb. 1865 [28-1865]

YOUNG, Mary Elizabeth.   See Mary Elizabeth Lewis.

* Originally published in the *Maryland Historical Magazine*. Reprinted here by permission of the Maryland Historical Society, Baltimore, MD.

Other Books by Mary K. Meyer:

*A Directory of Cayuga County Residents Who Supported
Publication of the History of Cayuga County, New York*

*Abstracts from Madison County, New York Newspapers
in the Cazenovia Public Library*

Baltimore City Birth Records, 1865–1894

Cemetery Inscriptions of Madison County, New York, Volume 1
Mary K. Meyer and Joyce C. Scott

*Free Blacks in Harford, Somerset and
Talbot Counties, Maryland 1832*

*Meyer's Directory of Genealogical Societies in the U.S.A.
and Canada: 1998–2000, 12th Edition*
Family of Mary K. Meyer

*Westward of Fort Cumberland: Military Lots Set Off for
Maryland's Revolutionary Soldiers*

Who's Who in Genealogy and Heraldry 1990
Mary K. Meyer and P. William Filby